MIND
STRETCHERS

ANGUS & ROBERTSON PUBLISHERS

Unit 4, Eden Park, 31 Waterloo Road,
North Ryde, NSW, Australia 2113, and
16 Golden Square, London W1R 4BN,
United Kingdom

First published in Australia
by Angus & Robertson Publishers in 1987
First published in the United Kingdom
by Angus & Robertson (UK) in 1987
Reprinted in 1988

Copyright © Geoffrey R. Marnell 1987

ISBN 0 207 15564 X

Typeset in 11/12 pt Goudy by
Midland Typesetters
Printed in Australia by The Book Printer

MIND
STRETCHERS

125 puzzles to tone up the muscles of
your mind

GEOFFREY R. MARNELL

Illustrations by Mark David

ANGUS
& ROBERTSON
PUBLISHERS

Introduction

Street joggers are such a common sight these days that they are much less frequently the object of jealous ridicule than they used to be. Those well-advertised diseases of indolence – and, perhaps, an obstinate bulge around the midriff – have taught us, instead, to respect these despisers of flab and inflexibility.

There is flab and inflexibility of another kind, too, a kind much easier to hide – especially from ourselves! A flabby mind – a mind that brings to a problem a great weight of irrelevance – and an inflexible mind – one lacking the suppleness to copy logic's leaps and twists – is one unlikely to climb with ease the stairs of thought, if it can climb them at all. Eventually, it may even prefer to remain on the ground floor of ideas, sharing with prejudice and intuition the scorn of nimbler minds, until finally the arteries of reason are clogged beyond repair.

What to do? Why not take a cue from the street joggers. Just as they have made a routine of exercising the muscles of the body, one can exercise the muscles of thought, so sharpening those faculties of reason and imagination that, if left untrained, will be impossibly slow to react to many of the problems that beset a lifetime.

On the pages that follow is a variety of puzzles or – what amounts to the same thing – exercises for the mind. In themselves they are not significant. No matter of great moment hangs on their solution. But they have a purpose beyond themselves, for they provide those whose minds have become a bit lazy with some badly needed exercise, as well as offering a little variety and amusement to those who do, or are trying to, keep their mind trim.

No single exercise demands any special skill or knowledge beyond that to be expected from a good general education. All you will need is a little imagination, a good deal of perseverance and a modicum of optimism. And if you find some puzzle particularly tormenting, so much the better. You can be sure, then, that your mind is getting a decent work-out.

The exercises are not in order of difficulty, so newcomers to the gymnasium of the mind should not be discouraged if they cannot lift the early weights. A guide to the difficulty of each puzzle appears after the solutions, each puzzle being rated on a scale of increasing difficulty from 1 to 10. The ratings are subjective, to some extent, for what one experienced puzzlist may find to be an excruciatingly difficult puzzle, another may find a condescension. Still, if the guide prevents unnecessary discouragement, it has earned its place in this book.

The solutions are not given in the same order as the puzzles, so that if readers should accidentally glance at the solution next in line to the one they are checking it will not spoil their pleasure in working out the next puzzle. The uniqueness, not to mention correctness, of the solutions is always a worry for authors of books like this. Let me just say that, at the time of printing, the judge's decision is final, but correspondence *will* gladly be entered into.

Geoffrey R. Marnell
Melbourne, 1987

Exercises

1 At 2 p.m. on 9 November, Mr Sailor set out from his private tropical island in a motor boat, bound for another island exactly 250 kilometres away. He set the throttle to give a speed of 50 kilometres per hour and, at that rate, had enough fuel for a 6 hour journey. He carried no sails which he could hoist in case of an engine failure, and, anyway, they would have been of no use, as there was a ferocious headwind blowing for the entire journey. He arrived at his destination at 6 p.m. on 10 November. Where was he boating?
Solution 36

2 After travelling the first 500 kilometres of a 1000 kilometre flight at an average speed of 500 kilometres an hour, how fast must a plane fly for the remaining 500 kilometres for its average speed for the whole trip to be 1000 kilometres an hour? *Solution 45*

3 A man walks 6 kilometres every day, without stopping, to the top of a hill and down again. He sets off with his dog, but, being somewhat long in the tooth, the dog can walk only half as fast as his master. Consequently, on his way down the hill, the man meets his dog still struggling up the hill. At this point, the dog turns round and follows the man home. How far does the dog end up walking?
Solution 24

4 Pauline, Colleen, Irene and Eileen are all university students, studying—in some order or another—medicine, arts, engineering and physics. They are also acknowledged sportswomen, and each represents her college in one or other of cricket, archery, rowing and swimming. The swimmer and the arts student live in a different college from Irene and the archer, while Eileen lives in the same college as the rower. In addition, Pauline and the medical student share a room in college, while Colleen and the engineering student have adjoining rooms. Finally, the medical student is just learning to swim. Who is studying what, and in what sport does each girl represent her college? *Solution 115*

5 If it takes me 2 minutes to walk up a moving escalator in the same direction as the escalator, but 6 minutes to walk—at the very same pace—down that same escalator, how much faster than the escalator am I walking?   *Solution 26*

6 Colonel McMuddlechump sent the following coded message: VMVNB ZGGZXPRMT, which, by the accepted code, read ENEMY ATTACKING. Shortly afterwards, he sent another message: ILRMUVIXLNLMGH MLLWLW, which Headquarters could not unravel; not, at least, until they received the following properly coded message: ELDVOH IVEVIHVW OZHG NVHHZTV. What was the Colonel's second message?   *Solution 99*

7 One prize contestants can win on the television game show "Finders Keepers" is gold bullion. All they need do is correctly pick which one of the 7 gold ingots is heavier than the other 6 identical ingots—and that ingot is theirs! To help them, they are provided with an old-fashioned balance-scale, but they must find the odd ingot in no more than two weighings. How could this be done? What if there were 8 ingots, with one heavier than the rest?   *Solution 60*

8 Joe's No-Nonsense Grocery Store is just what its name suggests! There is never a sale and never a discount for buying a quantity of any one line. This morning, Mrs Grundy bought 7 items from old Joe, paying exactly $9.99. The items were of two sorts, one sort costing exactly a dollar more than the other. What, then, was the price of each sort?   *Solution 55*

9 The enlightened government of a radical state is about to introduce solar-powered electricity generators to work in unison with the traditional coal-burning generators. The government has assured the electorate that this development will reduce electricity charges by 25%. In addition, the government plans to introduce computerised billing, and this, too, will reduce electricity charges by 25%. If a resident of this utopian state has been consistently charged $20 a month for her electricity, how much should she expect to pay under the new system?   *Solution 81*

10 Arrange three 2's so that the result is 16.   *Solution 28*

11 At sunrise on 1 December, the defending army could be said to have finally stopped the hitherto unchecked advance of the invaders, just under 12 kilometres inside their border. Straightaway they began their own offensive, having greatly strengthened their front-line troops. With superior fire power, they managed to push the invaders back 3 kilometres during the day, but the invaders, using guerilla tactics, managed to regain 2 kilometres in the course of the night. At this rate, of course, the invaders would soon be pushed back to the border. On – December, that was, in fact, what happened. (Fill in the blank.) *Solution 80*

12 Mrs Childlover had her first child at the age of 23, another a year later, and a third the year after that. How old will she be when her age is the same as the sum of her children's ages? *Solution 86*

13 Professor Horologer has 5 clocks in his sitting room, which, although they are set correctly each day at noon, do not keep very good time. He knows that in any one hour, one clock gains 6 minutes, another gains 8 minutes, another loses 4 minutes, a fourth loses 12 minutes and the last gains 10 minutes, but he has forgotten which gains or loses what. One evening, he sees that two of the clocks read 6.00 and 8.45. What, then, is the correct time? *Solution 91*

14 A philatelist spent precisely $1 on 3 cent, 5 cent and 10 cent stamps. How many stamps did she get if she got the most number possible for her dollar?   *Solution 43*

15 During the first 10 laps of a 20 lap bicycle race, Edmonds pedalled at an average of 2 kilometres an hour slower than Sturrock; but, for the remaining 10 laps, he pedalled at an average of 2 kilometres an hour faster than Sturrock. Who, if either, won the race?   *Solution 40*

16 France, Italy and England each entered three yachts in a yacht race. The winning boat would score 9 points, the second boat 8 points, the third 7, and so on, with the last boat home scoring only 1 point. The country that gained the highest aggregate score would win the race. It was some time after France's *Azure* had finally crossed the line as the last yacht home that the judges, studying photographs of the event, were able to separate Italy's *Fiorracio* and *Brio* (who both finished ahead of the other Italian yacht). However, when the scores for each country were totalled, they were found to be exactly the same. From which country, then, was the winning yacht, and what was the best place gained by an English yacht?

Solution 124

17 The words SIN, LINE and DEW can be formed from the letters of a 7 letter word. The words PATH and RACE can be formed from the letters of another 7 letter word. What are the words?

Solution 22

18 Which three letters continue the following sequence:

K U T S L M R Q N O P ...

Solution 32

And which two are left out of this sequence:

A Z B Y D W G T K - - K V E

Solution 126

19 An aircraft flies due north for 1000 kilometres and then due south for 2000 kilometres. It is then 3000 kilometres from its starting point. Where has it been flying? *Solution 89*

20 The *Spirit of Progress* pulls out of Central Station at 7 p.m. and arrives at Goulburn, 180 kilometres away, at 9 p.m. Throughout the journey, a frenzied fly has flown backwards and forwards along the full length of a 70 metre carriage at 60 kilometres an hour. How far has the fly travelled by the time the train has reached Goulburn? *Solution 38*

21 If 5 machines can make 1000 billy cans in four days, how many similar machines would be needed to make 1500 billy cans in just one day? *Solution 15*

22 Mrs Sweetmum spends exactly 17 cents each shopping day on lollies for her three children. They always get just three sorts of lollies: sherbert bombs (which cost 2 cents each), musk sticks (which are 1 cent each) and chocolate bullets (which are 3 for 2 cents). Moreover, the children always insist on, and get, more musk sticks than any other lolly. If Mrs Sweetmum divides the lollies equally, how many of each variety does she buy? *Solution 27*

chocolate bullets

Sherbert bombs

musk sticks

23 Mr Amneez, on gaining consciousness following a car crash, could not remember how old he was. He could, however, remember that he had 3 daughters born at five-yearly intervals, the oldest born when he was just 20. He also remembered that his youngest daughter had just had a birthday and was exactly half as old as the oldest daughter. How old is Amneez? *Solution 51*

24 Four students sat an examination, and their resulting marks were all whole numbers. Allan was top of the class and scored 80 marks more than the lowest-scoring student. Brian's mark had the very same two digits in it as Allan's. Chris's mark was a third of Allan's, and similarly, David's mark was a third of Brian's. Oddly enough, David's mark had the very same two digits in it as Chris's. What marks did the four boys get? *Solution 44*

25 Which two symbols continue the following sequence?

A 5 C 3 F 9 J 7 O 21 U 19 B 5 . . .

Solution 64

And which two are missing from this sequence?

24 – 21 U 1– R 15 O 12 L 9 I

Solution 127

Interrupted sequence

26 Place the numbers below into the matrix so that the sum of the numbers in each row, and in each column, is 23 and the sum of the numbers in each full diagonal is 22.

8 4 6 9 5 4 5 6 5 6 7 6 3 8 5   *Solution 3*

27 The members of an astronomical society decided to charter a plane so that they might get a better view of an approaching comet. The first 100 members to sign up for the trip were given a 25% discount off the standard fare. These early birds contributed 75% of the total cost of the fares, which amounted to $24,000. How many members went on the flight?   *Solution 29*

28 Before being called out of the classroom, a teacher wrote a perfectly correct subtraction on the blackboard. During his absence, some of his more mischievous pupils rearranged the figures in each line of the equation, creating the following incorrect subtraction:

$$
\begin{array}{r}
4\,9\,8 \\
-\,5\,7\,3 \\
\hline
=\,9\,0\,6
\end{array}
$$

On his return, the teacher realised what the students had done but was not particularly worried. In no time at all he was able to deduce what the original equation was. Can you?   *Solution 13*

29 Which word, HATRED or POPPED, continues the following sequence? And why?

CHIEF   LAUGH   HIJACK   PICKLE   HYMN . . .

Solution 9

And which of CREASED and TURN-OFF continues this sequence:

AMBLE   ABILITY   FACETS   MENDED   BURNER . . .

Solution 128

30 A contestant on a television games show is allowed to draw one note at a time from a barrel contining ten $5 notes, eight $10 notes, six $20 notes and five $50 notes until she has drawn four notes of the one denomination. What is the very most she can win?

Solution 21

31 Laughlin, Crowthers, Chomley and Rawlins are four new members of the Professionals' Club. One is a doctor, one is a teacher, the third is a dentist and the fourth is a barrister. Laughlin and Chomley were recently called as jurors to a trial in which the barrister acted as a counsel. Both Crowthers and the teacher have their teeth attended to by the dentist (who, having married Laughlin's sister, always gives him a discount). Moreover, the teacher had earlier taught both Laughlin and Rawlins. What is each man's profession?

Solution 100

32 The following puzzle is a fully worked multiplication in which each figure has been replaced with a letter of the alphabet. Can you deduce what the original figures were?

```
        O N E
        S O B
       ─────────
      S N A T
    T I T L
    O N E
   ───────────
    I N T A T
```

Solution 18

33 I am 25 years younger than my oldest brother. When the digits of his age are multiplied together, the result is my age; and when the digits of my age are added together, the result is the first digit of his age. How old am I? *Solution 72*

34 In reply to a simple algebraic equation set by their mathematics teacher, Alice declared the answer to be 89, Beatrice thought the answer was 111 and Claudette was sure it was 105. Each was, however, wrong. One student's answer was out by twice as much as another's answer, and another's was out by nine times as much as one of the other answers. Who came closest to getting the answer correct? *Solution 25*

35 At the Top Spin Tennis Club, the summer season lasts for 21 weeks. Each member plays just one match a week, and he or she is ranked according to the number of matches won as a percentage of the number of matches played. (For example, 3 wins from 4 matches would give a player a score of 75%.) At one stage last season, the secretary of the club had won 10 matches, while the treasurer had a rounded-off average of 81.81%. Who, if either, had won the most matches? *Solution 58*

36 Two outback explorers, Alice and Springs, came across a third explorer, who, having run out of drinking water, was near death. Alice and Springs had 12 litres and 8 litres of water respectively. As this was more than enough for them to reach the next waterhole, the three agreed to divide the water amongst them equally. For their trouble, the rescued explorer gave Alice and Springs 20 slices of cured beef, which they proceeded to divide fairly. How many slices did Springs get?   *Solution 69*

37 Professor Horologer likes to think that he has more time to finish his work than he really has. So he has set the four clocks in his study to be an average of exactly 2 hours slow. If two of the professor's clocks read 6.55, a third reads 6.42 and the fourth reads 6.28, what is the correct time?   *Solution 37*

38 The executives of All Australia Airlines are difficult masters! They proudly set the airline's timetable to show arrival times to the nearest minute and expect strict punctuality from their pilots. This is no easy task for the pilots, since, first, no allowance is made in the timetables for headwinds or tail winds that might affect the duration of flights, and, second, pilots are instructed to fly at full throttle at all times. No one, obviously, pays much attention to the airline's scheduled arrival times! At 7.30 one morning, an All Australia Airlines jet took off on time from Melbourne Airport bound for Sydney. It arrived there at 8.30. At 9.15, again on time, it took off for a return trip to Melbourne, arriving there at 10.45 after battling the same steady headwind it had taken advantage of on its way to Sydney. How late was the plane on arrival in Melbourne?   *Solution 103*

39 The day after the day preceding tomorrow week is 5 days after Tuesday. What day is it today?   *Solution 84*

40 In a week of record discoveries, the Commonwealth Chemical Research Laboratories synthesised six new but short-lived compounds, which they christened Poxyalic-10, Symochlorine, Dramoline, Glyco-acetyline, Ethylate and Trichotron. But in the flurry of creative activity, some the researchers' papers fell victim to a nitric acid spill. The researchers remembered that three of the new compounds were acidic, two alkaline and one was neither acidic or alkaline. They also remembered that Poxyalic-10 and Symochlorine were similar in this regard, as were Dramoline and Glyco-acetyline; while Dramoline and Ethylate were radically different, as were Symochlorine and Trichotron, and Poxyalic-10 and Ethylate. Which compounds, then, were acidic, which alkaline and which was neither acidic nor alkaline? *Solution 50*

41 Patrick McSoapie peddles washing detergent around the streets of Dublin from a large barrel on the back of a horse-drawn carriage. Mrs McAree and Mrs Flanagan stopped Patrick as he neared the end of his round one day, and both ordered a pint of detergent. At this late stage of the day, he had only an 8 pint, 5 pint and 3 pint container left, but he still managed to satisfy both orders, selling the detergent in the two smaller containers. How did he do it in just 12 separate pourings? *Solution 4*

42 Tom Muddlehead was off to the airport for his first-ever overseas holiday. After his taxi had gone 10 kilometres, he realised he had left his passport on the kitchen table at his mother's house. He got the cabbie to stop at a telephone booth, where he called his mother, asking her to bring the passport to the airport. His mother hurriedly got into her car and took off after the taxi. At the same time, Tom and the cabbie continued towards the airport. Tom's mother caught up with the taxi when they were 5 kilometres from the airport. With his passport safely pocketed, Tom continued to the airport, and his mother turned around and headed for home. When Tom arrived at the airport, his mother was still 10 kilometres from home. Assuming that the taxi and Tom's mother travelled at constant speeds over each section of their journey, can you work out how far Tom's mother lives from the airport? *Solution 109*

43 Complete the following puzzle as you would a normal cross-word – the only difference being that the answers are numbers, not words.

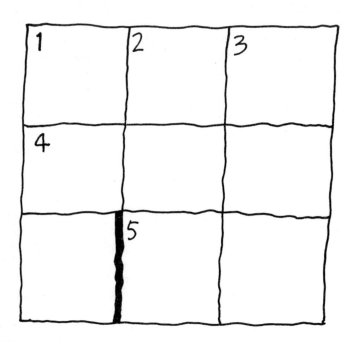

Across
1 The sum of all the digits is 7.
4 The square of an even number.
5 An exact divisor of 1 across.

Down
1 The sum of all digits is 3.
2 As 1 across.
3 An odd number.

(Hint: There are no zeros in any answer.)

Solution 16

44 Mr Craft, Mr Skill, Mr Art and Mr Wood are four school-teachers. Although each takes classes in just two subjects, only one of the four teaches mathematics. In addition:

a Three of the teachers take classes in English.
b Two take classes in history.
c Two of the four teach science.
d Peter does not teach English.
e Both Simon and Mr Skill teach history.
f Steven teaches science.
g Mr Craft does not teach the subjects Mr Art or Charles teaches.

From these facts, can you establish the full name of each teacher and the subjects he teaches?   *Solution 6*

45 The Kookawren Aviary prided itself on keeping only 30 birds in each of its pens. But when vandals cut through the wire enclosing 10 of the pens, the owners took the wise precaution of transferring the birds to other, more secure pens. This took the number of birds per pen to 40. How many birds did the aviary have all together?
                                                    Solution 66

46 Mensa, a club for the intellectually gifted, sets some pretty tough examinations for those seeking membership, as three professional people—Stewart, Campbell and Charles—recently found out. They are, in some order or other, a university lecturer, a surgeon and a lawyer, and the lecturer, who has a double doctorate in astrophysics, surprised everyone by failing the exam. Stewart, who, like Charles, has only a standard university education, just managed to pass, scoring only a few marks more than the struggling lawyer. What is each man's profession?   *Solution 71*

47 Which is the odd word out in the following list? And why?

AEROPLANE BUS TIMETABLE SPASM TRAGEDY

                                                    Solution 104

48 Unlike the common-or-garden variety of crossword, where the answers are, more often than not, synonyms of the clues, the answers in the following crossword puzzle may be synonyms *or* antonyms! Good luck.

Across
1 Doubtful
4 Slower
7 Likely
9 Friend
10 Starts
11 Finish
13 Concedes
14 Raced
15 Liberator
17 Best
19 Tired
20 Miserable
22 Bench
23 Freed
24 Hurry
25 Leaves

Down
1 Remunerated
2 Beautiful
3 Avoids
4 Cold
5 Lone
6 Elevated
7 Scarce
8 Abdicated
11 Underneath
12 Impure
15 Smooth
16 Withdraw
17 Civil
18 Teachers
21 Body
22 Dispatched

Solution 1

49 A father put aside $50 000 for his only son and future grandchildren. When the son reached his majority, the father gave him a certain amount of money, and when, a year later, the son married, he received a further $10 000. The father now found that he had only a third as much left for his grandchildren as he had following his first gift. How much did he have left?   *Solution 48*

50 Can you arrange the following numbers into pairs so that together the pairs form a regular arithmetic progression? (An example of a regular arithmetic progression is: 3, 6, 9, 12 . . .)

5 0 7 6 9 3 2 4 1 8

Solution 20

51 Hidden within the following square of letters is a well-known proverb, the letters of which, although all connected, are sometimes connected horizontally, sometimes vertically, and sometimes diagonally. Your task is to find the proverb hidden in the square. Beware: There may be the beginnings of more than one proverb!

Solution 8

52 The following puzzle is what could be called a "mathematical maze". You are to begin with the first encircled number, select a number adjacent to it, and try to reach, by division, subtraction, addition or multiplication, a number adjacent to the number you selected. If you are successful, draw a line between the three connecting numbers. Each line represents one move, and moves may be made horizontally, vertically or diagonally. You must find a path that connects the encircled numbers in *precisely* 14 moves, without doubling back on yourself.

③	5	12	6	14	20	19
4	7	1	5	3	17	39
7	9	12	7	2	4	12
2	4	9	4	7	14	21
15	10	5	13	16	21	3
15	20	25	9	4	3	7
3	5	8	17	7	10	④

Solution 17

53 Four countries each entered four players in a marbles competition. Each player in the competition was to play each player from the other three countries just once. On the world circuit, the English players were seeded 2nd, 8th, 14th and 20th; the French 1st, 12th, 15th and 19th; the American 5th, 6th, 11th and 18th; and the Australian 3rd, 4th, 16th and 17th. Which country would you expect to win the competition?   *Solution 5*

long division

54 The students who crept into Puzzle 28 have been at it again! While the teacher was out of the room, they vandalised a correct and completed long division on the blackboard, leaving visible only the 4's (of which there were exactly 4) and the 5's (of which there were exactly 5). Again, the teacher, on his return, changed the lesson from one of arithmetic to one of logic by showing the students how he could, by simple deduction *and not trial and error*, re-create the original division. Here is the blotted division for you to follow the teacher's example:

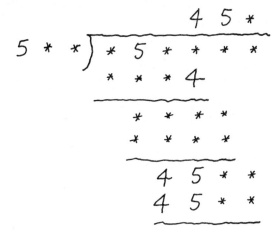

Solution 11

55 Ruritania was at war again. The King's Army desperately needed more guns, but there was little iron available from which to produce them. So the country's post offices were asked to rally round by contributing whatever weights they did not need to weigh parcels to the nearest kilogram. The post offices used old-style balance-scales to weigh parcels, and to that purpose had been issued with 1 kg, 2 kg, 3 kg, 7 kg, 9 kg, 10 kg, 15 kg and 20 kg weights. What is the maximum weight of metal each post office could contribute to the war effort and yet still be able to weigh parcels up to 20 kg in weight?   *Solution 2*

56 Can you make 3 English words by adding 4 letters – the same each time and in the same order – to the following word-endings?

----IC   ----ISH   ----ICITY

Solution 7

Can you do likewise by adding 2 letters to the following endings?

--EN   --ONG   --IGHT

Solution 129

57 The following figures represent three views of a cube, on the faces of which are the numbers 1 through to 6. What is the number missing from the third view?

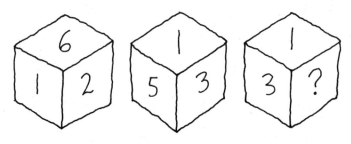

Solution 112

58 Of the residents of Babel Court, 3 speak Greek, Italian and English, 2 speak Greek and Italian, 7 speak English, 2 speak Italian and English, one speaks English and Greek, one speaks Italian only and 3 speak Greek only. How many residents are there altogether?

Solution 12

59 There are 5 stations on the Great Eastern Railway Line, not counting Flinders Street Station, from which all outward-bound trains depart. All Camberwell and Box Hill trains stop at Ringwood, while some Camberwell trains stop only at Box Hill and others only at Lilydale. All early-morning Belgrave trains stop at 4 stations on the way, while all off-peak Ringwood trains run express. Finally, all Box Hill trains stop at Lilydale. What, then, are the stations on the Great Eastern Railway Line in order of distance from Flinders Street Station? *Solution 34*

60 Hidden within this maze of letters are two well-known proverbs. Can you find them? (You may read in any direction, horizontally, vertically or diagonally. But beware: Not all the letters are used in the sayings!)

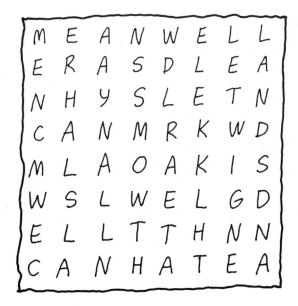

```
M  E  A  N  W  E  L  L
E  R  A  S  D  L  E  A
N  H  Y  S  L  E  T  N
C  A  N  M  R  K  W  D
M  L  A  O  A  K  I  S
W  S  L  W  E  L  G  D
E  L  L  T  T  H  N  N
C  A  N  H  A  T  E  A
```

Solution 14

61 Consider a six-digit number beginning with 2 and ending with 6. If the sum of all the digits together is 24, and the sum of the first three is one-third of the sum of the last three, what is the number?

Solution 31

62 Here is another crossnumber for you to nut out:

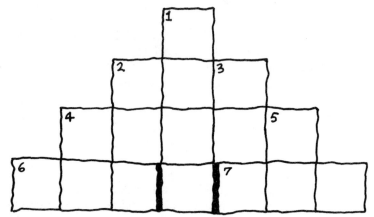

Across
2 The square of an odd number.
4 The sum of the digits equals 11.
6 A perfect square.
7 See 1 down.

Down
1 An odd number with digits adding to 6.
2 A number with equally ascending even digits.
3 A number with equally descending odd digits.
4 The sum of the digits equals 10.
5 The sum of the digits equals 3.

(Hint: There are no zeros in any answer.)

Solution 23

63 Three trains, A, B and C, are travelling along three parallel tracks. Each train is the same length as the others. A is travelling in the same direction as B and takes 24 seconds to overtake it. C is travelling in the opposite direction but is travelling at the same speed as A. It takes 8 seconds to pass B. How much faster than B is C travelling? And how long did it take A and C to pass each other?

Solution 42

64 Paul Bloom was a carefree student, who did not bother with his homework or his classroom study. Fed up with him getting all the answers wrong in class, his exasperated teacher decided to give Paul an ultimatum:

"Paul Bloom," he said, "I am going to give you one last chance. You may write on this sheet of paper one sentence–a sentence of your own choice–and if that sentence is wrong, Paul Bloom, you will be expelled from this school. But if it is correct, you may come back next term."

Paul wrote down his sentence and, just to prove that he had been listening, used only words that his teacher had used. The sentence–despite being grammatically perfect and free from spelling mistakes–quite baffled his teacher. He simply could not work out if it were right or wrong. For his ingenuity, Paul got to return next term. Can you think what Paul might have written?   *Solution 62*

65 Two salesmen, Gordon and Graeme, are always vying for the best daily commission (which is 20% on all goods sold priced at $5 or more). On a particular day, the only items for sale on which they could get a commission are priced at $20, $160, $640, $40, $5, $1280, $320, $80 and $10. At the end of that day, all these items had been sold, and Gordon's total commission was just $1 more than Graeme's. Who, then, sold the article priced at $160?

Solution 35

66 Sam and Thomas are competing in a swimming race being held over a number of lengths of a pool. Sam is soon shown to be a good deal faster than Thomas and is on his second length when, 10 metres from the far blocks, he passes Thomas, who is still on his first length. When Sam is on his third length and some 80 metres from the far blocks, he passes Thomas nearing the end of his second length. Assuming that both swimmers swam at constant speeds and did not pause at any end, how long is the pool?   *Solution 30*

67 Which two letters continue the following sequence?

        Z D G I I M P R R . . .

Solution 39

And which two are missing from this sequence?

A C E G – M P T X – G L

Solution 130

68 Doctors in Ruritania had been studying a new disease before their laboratory and all their research papers were destroyed in a war. The disease was characterised by six days of the following painful symptoms: a rash, fever, uncontrollable coughing and hallucinations. The doctors remembered that each symptom lasted for precisely one day, and that a day of fever never followed a day of coughing. Nor was the rash followed by fever, and the hallucinations – which always occurred early in the course of the disease – did not follow a day of the rash. They also remembered that the second day of the disease was characterised by coughing and the fourth by the rash. Can you, now, work out the exact course taken by the disease?

Solution 68

69 All but two of the numbers have been removed from the following magic square. Can you replace the numbers, while ensuring that the sum of each row, each column and each diagonal equals 12? (Note: No number is to be used more than once.)

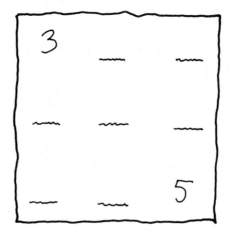

Solution 94

70 At the small round table just inside the door at Maxim's, Sachaverell, Algernon, Daphne and Chloe met together for a class reunion. Since leaving Stretchmind Grammar, they had each gone on to become a luminary in their chosen field. One had become a literary critic, another a flamenco guitarist, another a ventriloquist and the other an oenologist. The engaged couple—Algernon and Daphne—sat next to each other, and the ventriloquist sat opposite Sachaverell. On the right of the oenologist sat Chloe, and there was a woman to the left of the guitarist. Can you match the names with the professions? *Solution 41*

71 Five cricket commentators were given an opportunity to predict the outcome of a World Series Cup competition. Clive Stumping thought the West Indies would win, with Australia second and England fifth. Richie Wrongun predicted a win to Australia, with the West Indies second and England fourth. Iain Capelli was certain the West Indies would win, with India third and Pakistan last. The patriotic Krishnan Murti placed India first, with England next and the West Indies last. Finally, Greg Tony thought England would scrape in overall winners, with Pakistan second and the West Indies not far behind in third place. Thanks to green wickets and a ward of injuries, it turned out to be a surprisingly unpredictable series, with each commentator making only one successful prediction. Which commentator came closest to predicting the result of the competition? *Solution 56*

72 In the following sequence, one of the numbers is wrong. Which one is it? And what should it be?

$$7 \quad 11 \quad 17 \quad 31 \quad 47 \quad 67 \quad 91 \ldots$$

Solution 77

And what is the missing number in the following sequence?

$$23 \quad 58 \quad 13 \quad 94 \quad 12 \quad 13 \quad ?3 \quad 34 \quad 88$$

Solution 133

73   The following four statements—only two of which are true—are about a married couple with two natural children:

a Peter is older than Colin.   **c** Susan is the mother.
b Anne is older than Susan.   **d** Peter is married to Anne.

Who is the mother, who the father, who the son and who the daughter?   *Solution 73*

74   Thomas Slowboy was born 5 years after his sister, Odette. Some years later, it was noted that Odette had had 5 times as many birthdays as Thomas. How old was Odette then?

Solution 46

75   The following number is composed of two other numbers mixed together, but mixed in such a way that the order of the figures in each number is preserved. One number is exactly half the other number. What are the two numbers?

36,749,298

Solution 49

76   In the following portmanteau-word, there are two other English words jumbled together (though jumbled in such a way that the order of the letters in each word is preserved). One word is an antonym of the other. Can you find both words?

SEXEPCORESTED

Solution 59

77   Archimedes once again took to his bath in search of new discoveries. But this day, all he could find to exercise his curiosity was the regularity of the drops of water dripping from the tap. He noted that it took precisely 2 seconds for 2 drops to fall. How long, then, should it take for 4 drops to fall from Archimedes' tap?

Solution 87

78 Harry Hydrophile loves splashing about in his new marble-bottomed below-ground swimming pool. He is so proud of it that he changes the water in it every single day. Using the tap in his back garden, Harry finds that he can fill the pool in a minimum of 30 minutes. But if he runs a hose from the tap inside his laundry to the pool, he can fill it in just 20 minutes. The pressure in the pipes at the front of his house is even better, so much so that a hose from the front tap to the pool does the job in just 12 minutes. Assuming that the water pressure from a tap is not reduced if any other tap is open, how long should it take Harry to fill his pool if all three taps were called into play at the same time?

Solution 82

79 A clock that loses 10 minutes every hour is set correctly at 10.00. What is the correct time when the clock next reads 10.00?

Solution 95

80 Starting with the word LACE, form a new English word by changing just one letter, and keep doing so with each new word until the *fourth* new word you form is SILK. When you have succeeded, try again, but change *two* letters each time.

Solution 121

81 A good Irish couple decided to take stock of their offspring after the birth of what they hoped would be their last child. They discovered that each son had as many brothers as one quarter of the total number of their children. In addition, each daughter had twice as many sisters as she had brothers. How many children did the couple have?

Solution 61

82 A jogger sets out fresh one morning and, with a good tail wind, averages 20 kilometres an hour between his home and the point at which he turns back. Being now a little weary and facing a headwind, he finds he can average only 12 kilometres an hour on the return leg (which, incidentally, follows the same route as the outward leg). What is his average speed for the whole run?

Solution 83

83 The mixing machine at Be-Vital Health Foods Pty Ltd is controlled by 5 switches numbered 1 to 5. A console above the switches is composed of a series of lights, which highlight which particular substance is being mixed. The console is arranged like this:

Add Iron	Add Copper	Add Niacin	Neutral	Add Sodium	Add Calcium	Add Vitamins	Add Phosphorus

At the beginning of each mixing session, the neutral position is highlighted, and the person responsible for the mixing, by using the switches, can cause the various substances listed on the console to be added to the mixing vat. Switch 1 brings about the action one position to the left of the action highlighted on the console; switch 2 two positions to the right; switch 3 three positions to the right; switch 4 four positions to the left; and switch 5 two positions to the left. At the end of each mixing session, the neutral position must once again be highlighted. What sequence of switches must be thrown in order to produce, in the shortest possible time, a mixture of niacin, sodium, iron, vitamins and copper, given that the sodium must be added to the vat before the vitamins?

Solution 75

84 Old Joe Crankety, purveyor of fine paints, decided to have his first sale in 25 years of trading. Not one to overdo things, Crankety told his assistant to put just three varieties on special: a satin, a gloss and a matt; and the colours were to be white, cream and beige. Never having held a sale before, Crankety was unsure how to price his specials, so he told his assistant to do this for him. As long as the satin paint was $1.95 more than the matt, the cream twice as much as the beige, and the beige three times the price of the white, old Crankety would, he said, accept whatever prices his assistant came up with. There were just two provisos: no price was to be lower than the 50 cents Crankety pays his wholesaler for each can of paint, and there were to be no special discounts for multiple purchases. What prices did the assistant put on the specials? And which colour matched which finish?   *Solution 106*

85 The initiation ceremony for those intrepid souls seeking membership to the Imbibers' Club can be a stomach-turning event. In one of the many rites of passage, the master of ceremonies arranges 9 glasses of liquor in a circle. (By tradition, he first places down a glass of gin and then—continuing clockwise—glasses of Lillet, vodka, rum, whisky, Drambuie, brandy, Cointreau and tequila.) The newcomer is then expected, in just 9 seconds, to select a glass, drain it and then drain every ninth glass in the circle until all the glasses are empty. He must, moreover, drink the Cointreau last. If, by some miscalculation, the initiate finds that he has some drink other than the Cointreau as the last drink to down, the master of ceremonies puts out another 9 glasses, and the newcomer must—if he is still standing—try again!

As you might imagine, the club is not too keen on publicity. But it did make the front page of the *Times* back in the 1930s, when Bertie Wooster, despite a heavy meal of Lobster Thermidor and cheesecake at the Drones Club only minutes before, took up the club's challenge. For Bertie was the very first to pass the test in just one round; and the press was impressed.

"What drink did you start with," they all wanted to know. But the pride of the Woosters is such that Bertie steadfastly remained mute on that point. All he would say was that drinking the Lillet before the whisky was all that saved him from certain digestive catastrophe.

All the journalists reported Bertie's medical advice, but not one managed to deduce from it the answer to the question of which drink Bertie started with. Can you?   *Solution 98*

86 Be-Vital Health Foods Pty Ltd (introduced in Puzzle 83) have discovered a new compound, which, they say, cures the common cold. It is a mixture of vitamins, sodium, copper, iron, niacin and calcium. One day the company's mixing machine—as described in the earlier puzzle—went on the blink, with only 2 of its 5 mixing switches working. Nonetheless, the company was still able to mix up its new wonder drug. What sequence of just 7 switches enabled them to do so?   *Solution 113*

87 Rearrange the numbers in the following square so that no number appears more than once in any row, column or diagonal.

1	2	3	4
2	3	4	1
3	4	1	2
4	1	2	3

Solution 118

88 In a round-robin cricket competition between Australia, England, India and New Zealand, each team played each other team just once. A team was awarded 10 points for a win, 5 for a draw and none for a loss. There were only 2 draws in the competition, which saw New Zealand outright winners (with 2 wins, and a loss to India) and Australia outright losers. What was the result of each match?

Solution 110

89 Can you break up the following number into groups of smaller numbers, without changing the order of the figures, so that the *sum* of all the groups is equal to the square of the first group?

123 456 789

Solution 74

90 Being reluctant to embrace high-technology without being sure of its merits, the manager of a secretarial office managed to get hold of some word-processing machines to run a trial. She found that 6 word-processing machines together with 3 electric typewriters could produce as much work in 4 days as 4 word-processing machines and 4 typewriters could produce in 5 days. Which piece of equipment—the word processor or the electric typewriter—is the most productive? And how much more productive is it?   *Solution 90*

91 As part of its plan to upgrade the rail system, a progressive state has bought some new, high-speed trains. To help defray the cost of these trains, the government has decided to change the fare structure. Instead of charging according to the distance a passenger wants to travel—as was past practice—the government has decided to set the fares according to the scheduled speed of a train, with a passenger on board a faster train paying more than a passenger on a slower train. In order to get to work, I have to change trains for the last quarter of my journey, and, alas, that leg is by means of an old rail-motor that is soon to get a telegram from the Queen! That leg takes, in fact, twice as long as the first leg (if, that is, both legs are according to schedule). If I pay $1.20 for the first leg of my journey, how much should I pay for the second leg under the government's new pricing policy?   *Solution 85*

92 In an attempt to outwit their teacher once and for all, the mischievous students from Puzzle 28 replaced each figure in a multiplication with a letter. Fortunately, they gave each figure just the one letter; but, much to their dismay, the teacher was once again able to re-create the original multiplication. Can you? Here is the students' version:

$$
\begin{array}{r}
E\ C\ K \\
C\ B \\
\hline
C\ C\ B\ K \\
M\ K\ L \\
\hline
F\ B\ B\ K
\end{array}
$$

Solution 101

93 An outback explorer managed to walk across a desert 280 kilometres wide. What is extraordinary about this feat is that he could carry only 4 days' rations and could walk only 40 kilometres a day. Moreover, given the harsh desert conditions, he could not have survived a day without a full day's rations. He completed the crossing in 27 days. How did he do it?   *Solution 57*

94 John, Chris, Paul and Donald drive either a Holden or a Ford. John and Chris drive the same make of car, but John's car is different from Paul's. If Paul drives a Ford, then Donald does not drive a Holden, but if Paul drives a Holden, then so does Chris. Who drives which make of car?   *Solution 63*

95 At the Uppercrust gentlemen's club the other day, Mr Bluechip, Mr Silverspoon, Sir James Blueblood and Mr Risingstar were each bragging about how little tax they had paid in the last financial year. They were, in some order or other, an orthopaedic surgeon, a stockbroker, a Queen's Counsel and a director of a large public company. They had all paid exact dollars, and the director had paid half as much tax as the Queen's Counsel, with the orthopaedic surgeon paying twice as much as the Queen's Counsel but half as much as the stockbroker. Mr Silverspoon, although paying twice as much tax as Mr Bluechip, could, with some justification, brag to his friends – or at least one of them – while the knighted member was not happy, having paid $2731. What is each man's occupation?   *Solution 76*

96 With his grand tax savings, Sir James Blueblood (introduced in the previous puzzle) decided to buy a parcel of grazing land. He also bought 6 railings of equal length, to be used to form cattle enclosures. (They were comb-like railings, which could be clipped over one another at pretty well any point along their length.) Blueblood erected the railings as shown in the following diagram:

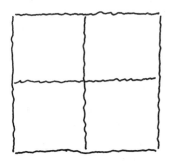

His good mate Mr Silverspoon – ever the braggart – laughed at Blueblood's enclosures, pointing out that, as the size of each enclosure was not important, he could have made 6 enclosures with the 6 railings instead of Blueblood's 4. Silverspoon constructed the 6 enclosures, and both men were happy – at least until the following weekend, when Mr Bluechip paid Sir James a visit. Bluechip smugly pointed out that with 6 railings, 7 enclosures could be built! How could the 6 railings be arranged to yield 6, and 7, enclosures? (Models made from matches may help you solve this puzzle, and note that no railing may be cut to a shorter length.) *Solution 114*

97 Lucky Jim went into his local confectionery shop to buy a chocolate bar. He paid 50 cents for the bar, and to his delight and astonishment, got back four times the change to which he was entitled. He noted that this was equivalent to twice the amount he tendered for the bar. What was Jim's total profit from the transaction? *Solution 65*

98 Of the 50 staff at a rather well-to-do private school, only 7 had just a bachelor's degree. Of the others, 24 had a master's degree as well, and 20 had a doctorate. How many had both a master's degree and a doctorate? *Solution 92*

99 A father has 11 children, to whom he distributes exactly $9 a week in pocket money. Having been persuaded of the virtues of positive discrimination, he makes a point of giving each son 50 cents a week, while each daughter receives $1 a week. How many sons and how many daughters does he have?   *Solution 108*

100 Two numbers in the following sequence have been omitted. Can you work out what they are?

3 6 5 9 ? 12 9 15 ?

Solution 119

And which two in the following sequence are wrong?

64 82 100 122 144 169 196

Solution 131

101 Allan, Bruce, Colin and David each began a game of poker with $7 made up solely of 20 cent pieces. At the end of the game, they each added up their coins. They found that Allan and David together had as many coins as Bruce and Colin together. Moreover, Allan had 2 coins more than Colin and David together, while Bruce and David together had 8 coins more than the other two together. What was each player's profit (or loss) from the game?
Solution 53

102 Adam, James and Charles are three members of the Biceps gymnasium. Each plays two sports out of cricket, baseball, football, soccer, rugby and tennis, but no one plays a sport played by another. Charles and the cricketer work together, and the three travel to the gym together, Adam (who despises baseball), the cricketer and the soccer player taking it in turns to drive. Charles, the footballer (who does not play tennis), and the tennis player (who does not play cricket) all went to the same school. Who plays which sports?
Solution 96

103 Rearrange the numbers in the following square so that no number appears more than once in any row, column or diagonal.

Solution 111

104 Professor Horologer (introduced in a couple of earlier puzzles) had such a penchant for clocks that he took to repairing them himself. He was quite successful at his new-found hobby, but one day, after fixing the difficult insides of an antique grandfather clock, he put the hands on back-to-front, so that the hour hand behaved like the minute hand should and vice versa. Instead of correcting his mistake, he did a quick calculation and noted down the times when the clock would still show the correct time. If the professor set the clock correctly at midday, how many times in the next 12 hours will it show the correct time? *Solution 67*

105 During his 27 day trek, the outback explorer introduced in Puzzle 93 had plenty of time to reflect on the difficulties he had experienced in ensuring sufficient supplies for his entire trip. A few calculations made him realise that had he used the local natives to carry some of his supplies, he could have completed the 280 kilometre cross-desert trek in just 7 days: a saving of nearly 3 weeks! What is the minimum number of bearers the explorer would need to employ in order to make the crossing in just 7 days, given that, as before, only 40 kilometres can be travelled in any one day and only 4 days' supplies can be carried by any one man, and given also that explorer and bearer alike need a full day's rations every day? (Assume, in this puzzle, that extreme climatic conditions would make it impossible for supplies to be safely cached along the way.)

Solution 117

106 Four jockeys, Clive, Alf, Mick and Darren, were filling in time between engagements by larking about on the steward's scales. They discovered that Clive and Alf together do not weigh as much as Mick and Darren together. Moreover, Alf and Darren weigh more than Mick and Clive. Oddly enough, Alf and Mick weigh precisely the same as Clive and Darren. Who is the heaviest, and who the lightest, jockey? *Solution 78*

107 At a party, you are asked to draw 12 balls from a bag of 30 red balls and place them in a bag containing 60 black balls. You then thoroughly mix the balls in the second bag before being blindfolded and withdrawing 12 balls from it, which you place in the bag of red balls. How many more black balls would you expect to find in the first bag (the bag that initially contained only red balls) than red balls in the second bag? *Solution 93*

108 "Did you take the eclair from the refrigerator?" demanded Johnny's mother.

"No, Mum. It was your only cousin's only aunt's only grandchild who took it."

Assuming that Johnny was telling the truth, who stole the eclair?

Solution 33

109 The following represents a correct long division in which each figure has been replaced by a letter of the alphabet (with just one letter representing any one number). Can you *deduce* the figures in the original long division?

```
          D  C  K
  B K ) C  F  H  G
        B  K
        E  D  H
        D  F  C
              E  C  G
              E  C  G
```

— *Solution 116*

110 I have 4 pieces of string labelled A, B, C and D. Pieces A and B end-to-end are not as long as D alone, while pieces B and D together are longer than pieces A and C together but shorter than D and C. If pieces A and D are equal in length to pieces B and C, and if the smallest piece is 1 centimetre shorter than the second smallest piece, how much shorter than the longest piece is the second longest piece? *Solution 102*

111 Three known criminals—Simpkins, Humphreys and Dagge— were rounded up following a daring daylight robbery. Predictably, each denied responsibility for the robbery, and in addition, each made just one further statement. Simpkins alleged that Dagge did it, while Dagge told the superintendent that his good mate Humphreys was not involved in the robbery. Humphreys was equally loyal to his good buddy Simpkins, declaring his innocence to the superintendent. If only one of each man's two assertions is true, and if only one of the three is responsible, who committed the robbery? *Solution 79*

112 Three clocks in Professor Horologer's study show the time as 1.50, 2.10 and 2.16. The clocks are neither all fast nor all slow. But they are all wrong, and wrong by an average of 13 minutes. What is the correct time? *Solution 97*

113 Graeme, Frank, John and Iain were playing a new game of cards that required them to form 2 teams of 2 players each and attempt to win as many of the 26 tricks per game as possible. At the end of one game, Graeme had the most tricks, Frank had 2 tricks fewer than his partner, John had 5 tricks more than his lowest-scoring opponent, and Iain had half as many tricks as his highest-scoring opponent. Who partnered whom, and how many tricks did each player win? *Solution 88*

114 Which of the offered solutions, labelled A to E, continues the following sequence of shapes?

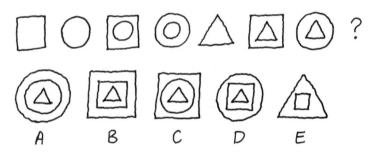

A   B   C   D   E

Solution 19

115 Can you decipher the following coded message? (Hint: The message explains how it is to be deciphered!)

UI2 W4X2MT 30 UI3T N2TT1H2
1S2 S2QS2T2OU2E CZ O5NC2ST
1OE UI2 D4OT4O1OuT I1W2 C22O
S2QM1D2E CZ UI2 O2YU M2UU2S
3O UI2 1MQI1C2U.

Solution 54

116 Mr Greatcharm celebrated his sixty-ninth birthday by marrying for the fourth time. Despite his repeated enquiries, his wife-to-be had been rather secretive about her age. On their wedding night she finally gave in, but in a very cryptic manner! She told Greatcharm that the sum of her present age and the number of his previous wives is equal to one-third of what his age will be when he is older by as many years as she is now. How old is she?

Solution 47

117 Four children go into a lolly shop. The first pays 20 cents for 3 musk sticks and 6 jubes. The second pays 12 cents for 4 aniseed balls and 2 musk sticks. The third pays 16 cents for 6 chewies, a musk stick and 2 aniseed balls. How much, then, should the fourth child have to pay for 2 musk sticks, 2 aniseed balls, 2 jubes and 2 chewies? *Solution 105*

118 With just two sand-glasses at your disposal—one emptying in 9 minutes and the other in 5—how could you tell when 11 minutes had elapsed? *Solution 107*

119 A keen punter places $30 on Omen Bet in the first race at Hanging Rock and the rest of his money on Hot Feet. Omen Bet tosses his jockey near the home turn, but Hot Feet wins easily, and the punter doubles the money he had bet on her. In the next race, the punter puts $30 on the favourite and the rest of his money on Lucky Horseshoe. The favourite is nipped on the line by Lucky Horseshoe, and the punter finds he has tripled the money he had placed on the colt. In the third race, he puts $30 on Wish Me Luck and the rest of his money on Bred For Speed. Bred For Speed lives up to her name and swamps the rest of the field. The punter quadruples the money he had on her and finds that he now has $240 in his pocket. How much money did he start with?

Solution 122

120 Those mischievous mathematics students introduced in earlier puzzles have now extended their campaign of disruption to their English classes. Before being called out of the classroom, their English teacher wrote a sentence concerning English grammar on the blackboard. During her brief absence, her playful charges rearranged the letters in the sentence. (They did, however, preserve the correct number of letters in each of the words.) The result was this:

B RANT AN W TIAP CORRESSDOVER GIENIE

Can you work out what the original sentence was?

Solution 70

121 Bernadette, Colleen and Dominique were sharing a bottle of Dom Perignon with three young men they had just met at the Melbourne Cup. In response to the men's curiosity about each woman's age, the three replied thus:

Bernadette: "I must admit to being older than Dominique."
Dominique: "Well, you are twenty-two, remember."
Colleen: "No. Bernadette's only twenty-one."
Bernadette: "But Colleen, you're a year older than I am."
Dominique: "She can't be, because Colleen is a year younger than I am."
Colleen: "I am, in fact, three years younger than Bernadette."

Dominique: "Yes, but I'm only nineteen."
Bernadette: "No, you're not. You're twenty."
Colleen: "Still, Dominique is older than I am."

Understandably, the three gentlemen were quite baffled, at least until the women admitted that they had each told one lie. How old, then, are the women? *Solution 123*

122 Which of the following 5 sentences are true?

a It is not the case that 2 consecutive sentences are both false.
b There are fewer false than true sentences.
c It is not the case that 3 consecutive sentences are all false.
d It is not the case that 2 consecutive sentences are both true.
e There are exactly 3 false sentences.

Solution 120

123 Five students sat two examinations, and when the results of the two examinations were totalled, Andrew was clearly the dux. This was a little surprising, since he was placed only third in both the English and the mathematics exams. Bernard topped the class in the English exam, and Edwina, though expected to top the class in the mathematics exam, came only fourth. Davina scored 15 marks more than Andrew in mathematics, but Andrew bettered Catherine by 15 marks in English. Given that there were no equal places in either examination, can you rank the 5 students in each examination? *Solution 125*

124 Which is the odd number out in the following list? And why?

87 111 78 92 51 36 24

Solution 52

And which are the odd words in this list:

TRY MATE RUBBER GOAL SOCCER RUN CHESS

Solution 132

125 Four of the government's brightest backbenchers were called into the Prime Minister's office. For their dedication and party loyalty, each was to be made a minister of one of four newly created portfolios. After the meeting with the Prime Minister, one of the four, Mr Chipley, was met by a group of journalists eager to find out who got which portfolio. One of the journalists asked:

"Is it true, Mr Chipley, that you have been made Minister for Pensioner Education, that Mr Adderson is now Minister for Public Relations, Mr Blitherer Minister for Popular Culture and Mr Deamon is Minister for New Technology?"

"That's not a very good prediction," replied Chipley.

"Well, then," another asked, "is Mr Adderson the Minister for New Technology, Mr Blitherer Minister for Pensioner Education, Mr Deamon Minister for Popular Culture and yourself the new Minister for Public Relations?"

"You are getting warmer," replied a teasing Chipley.

Yet another voiced a prediction:

"I've heard, sir, that you were given the Popular Culture portfolio, that Adderson is the new Minister for Pensioner Education, Blitherer has got the Public Relations job and Deamon will head the Ministry of New Technology. Is that how the Prime Minister allocated the new portfolios?"

"You are warmer still," said Chipley, motioning to his chauffeur. "But I must ask you to wait until the Prime Minister himself announces the new appointments. All I'm willing to say at this stage is that, no, I was not given the Popular Culture portfolio."

What portfolio was Chipley given?   *Solution 10*

Solutions

Solution 1 (Puzzle 48)

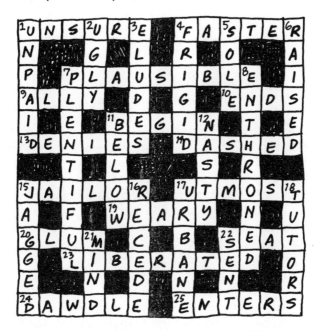

Solution 2 (Puzzle 55)

The correct answer is 44 kg. Each post office would need only the 1 kg, 3 kg, 9 kg and 10 kg weights. The trap for the unwary in this puzzle is to fail to see that the weights do not have to go into the same balancing tray. For example, if an article were a little over 8 kg, the article *together with* the 1 kg weight would just outweigh the 9 kg weight in the opposite tray. By taking out the 1 kg weight, the mail clerk would see that the item did not weigh more than 9 kg. (And, by judging the relative heights of the trays, the clerk could see – if this were necessary – that the item was closer to 8 kg than to 9 kg.)

Solution 3 (Puzzle 26)

8	4	5	6
4	5	5	9
6	6	6	5
5	8	7	3

Solution 4 (Puzzle 41)

a Patrick first filled the 3 pint container and then transferred the contents to the 5 pint container. (2 pourings)

b He then refilled the 3 pint container and poured as much of its contents as possible into the 5 pint container. This would have left exactly 1 pint in the 3 pint container, which he then transferred to the 8 pint container. (3 pourings)

c He next returned the contents of the 5 pint container to the barrel that held his bulk supply and filled the 3 pint container yet again. The contents of the 3 pint container were then transferred to the now empty 5 pint container. (3 pourings)

d The 3 pint container was filled again, and the 5 pint container was filled from the 3 pint container. This left 1 pint in the 3 pint container. The contents of the now full 5 pint container were transferred back to the bulk supply, and the pint in the 8 pint container was transferred to the 5 pint container. The net result is a pint of detergent in both the 3 pint and 5 pint containers. (4 pourings, making 12 in all)

Solution 5 (Puzzle 53)

Given those rankings, you would expect Australia to win the competition, with 26 wins out of 96 games, with America second (with 25 games), England third (23 games) and France last (22 games). It is a fallacy merely to add each country's rankings and select the country with the lowest aggregate score (a method that would give Australia and America a tie). Rather, you should list out all possible games (E1 v F1, E1 v F2, E1 v F3 and so on) and award each game to the better-seeded player.

Solution 6 (Puzzle 44)

1 Peter Craft teaches mathematics and science.
2 Charles Skill teaches history and English.
3 Simon Art also teaches history and English.
4 Steven Wood teaches science and English.

A *few hints:* From statements **a, d** and **g,** it follows that Peter is Mr Craft. From **d** and **e** (together with the fact that each teacher takes classes in just two subjects), it follows that neither Simon nor Steven teaches mathematics. Hence, given that only one of the four teaches mathematics, that teacher must be either Charles or Peter. If you assume that Charles is the mathematics teacher and allocate the subjects accordingly, you will find that Charles's surname is Art. But from clue **g,** this is impossible. Consequently, Peter must be the mathematics teacher. Now, since Peter does not teach English, his other subject must be history or science. But if you assume that Peter teaches history, in allocating the remaining subjects according to the clues, you will find that Simon's surname must be Skill. But this is disallowed by clue **e.** Thus Peter's other subject is science. From here, the rest is plain sailing.

Solution 7 (Puzzle 56, Part A)

The 4 letters required can only be PUBL, making the 4 partly spelt words:

PUBLIC   PUBLISH   PUBLICITY

Solution 8 (Puzzle 51)
There is no fool like an old fool.

Solution 9 (Puzzle 29, Part A)
POPPED – because it, and not HATRED, continues the sequence of adjacent letters found in the other words, i.e. EF, GH, IJ, KL, MN and so on.

Solution 10 (Puzzle 125)
Chipley was given the New Technology portfolio. One way to approach this puzzle is to recognise that the 3 predictions made are progressively closer to the truth. Moreover, since on Chipley's own admission, he was not given the Popular Culture portfolio, one of the 4 statements in the last prediction is wrong. Hence the maximum number of correct statements in any prediction is 3. The predictions, then, could contain:

a 0, 1 and 2; or
b 0, 1 and 3; or
c 0, 2 and 3; or
d 1, 2 and 3 correct statements respectively.

Now, if the last prediction contained 3 correct statements, the fact that no two statements in that prediction are shared with the second prediction rules out possibilities **c** and **d**. Moreover, since Deamon was thought to have been given the New Technology portfolio in both the first and third predictions, and since the statement about Chipley in the third prediction is wrong, it cannot be the case that the first prediction had no correct statements and the third 3 correct statements. This rules out possibilities **b** and **c**. The one remaining possibility is **a**.

Now, if the first prediction is wrong in all cases, Deamon cannot have been given the New Technology portfolio. Since this statement is shared with the third prediction, it follows that the remaining 2 statements in the third prediction are correct: Adderson got the Pensioner Education portfolio and Blitherer Public Relations. It then follows that the only statement in prediction 2 that could be correct is that which gives Deamon the Popular Culture portfolio. This leaves Chipley with New Technology.

Solution 11 (Puzzle 54)

a Because the last digit in the first multiplication and the first digit of the answer are both 4, the last digit of the divisor must be either 1 or 6.

b If the last digit of the divisor were 1, then, because the second digit of the answer is 5, the last digit of the second multiplication would also have to be 5. Because it is not, the last digit of the divisor must be 6.

c Because the third multiplication yields a figure greater than 4500, the last digit of the answer (which is multiplied by the divisor to give this figure) must be greater than 7.

d The last digit of the answer cannot be 9, for then the last digit of the third multiplication would end in a 4, which it does not. Therefore the last digit of the answer is 8, making the answer 458.

e Because the last part of the third multiplication yields 40, and yet the first two digits of the answer to the third multiplication are 45, there must be a carry-over of 5 from the second part of the third multiplication. In other words, 8 multiplied by the middle digit of the divisor, plus the carry-over (which in this case must be 4) must yield a figure in the fifties. The only possibility for this middle digit is, then, 6.

f The divisor is, then, 566, and the answer 458. Multiplying these out gives 259 228, after which the remaining figures can be got by following through the division. The complete solution is:

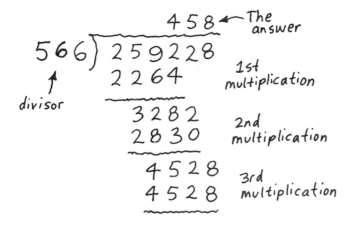

Solution 12 (Puzzle 58)

There are 13 residents. If you total the number of residents who, by the clues, speak only one language and those who speak a number of languages, the result is 12. But in that number, you would have counted only 6 English-speaking residents. We are told, however, that 7 speak English. So there is an additional resident, one who speaks English but not Italian or Greek. This makes 13 residents in all.

Solution 13 (Puzzle 28)

$$
\begin{array}{r}
9\,8\,4 \\
-\,3\,7\,5 \\
\hline
=\,6\,0\,9
\end{array}
$$

Solution 14 (Puzzle 60)

Many hands make light work.
All's well that ends well.

Solution 15 (Puzzle 21)

If 5 machines can make 1000 cans in 4 days, they would make 250 cans in one day, which is equivalent to 50 cans per machine. So 30 machines would be needed to make 1500 cans in just one day.

Solution 16 (Puzzle 43)

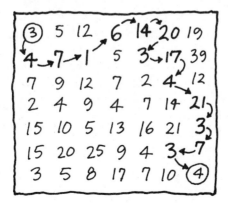

a Since there are no zeros in any answer, 1 down can only be 111.
b Hence 4 across can only be 144 (12^2) or 196 (14^2). If it were 196, then the digits in 2 down would total more than 7. So 4 across must be 144.
c It follows that 2 down can be only 241 or 142, and 1 across can be only 124 or 115 respectively.
d If 2 down is 241 and 1 across is 124, then 5 across must divide exactly into 124, begin with 1 and be odd. But not one of 11, 13, 15, 17 or 19 divides exactly into 124. Therefore, 2 down must be the other alternative, i.e. 142. In addition, 1 across must be 115 and 5 across must be odd and begin with 2.
e The only odd number in the twenties that divides exactly into 115 is 23, this being the answer to 5 across.

Solution 17 (Puzzle 52)

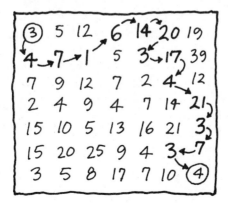

Solution 18 (Puzzle 32)

The correct solution is:

$$
\begin{array}{r}
564 \\
153 \\
\hline
1692 \\
2820 \\
564 \\
\hline
86292 \\
\end{array}
$$

One way to approach this puzzle is as follows:

a Because rows 1 and 5 are identical, S = 1.

b If A = A + L in the second addition, L must equal 0.

c If L = 0, then either O or E must equal 5. If E = 5, then T must equal 0 or 5 (since T = E × B). But L = 0, and *both* T and E cannot equal 5; so O must equal 5.

d If 5 × E must equal 0, then E must be an even number. If E is even, so too must be B × E. Hence T must also be even.

e The fourth addition must have a carry-over (since it ends with an N, and N appears within the addition). This carry-over can only be 1 (since, given that the maximum N or I can be is 9, the sum cannot exceed 18). Consequently, in the fifth addition, I = T + 1 (the carry-over) + 5 (the value of O).

f Since T cannot be 0 or 1, and since I must be 9 or less, T can only be 2 or 3 to satisfy the equation at **e** above. But T must be an even number (see **d** above). So T = 2, and, following on, I = 8.

g Because L = 0, there can be no carry-over from the second addition. Morever, there must be a carry-over from the third addition, which can only be 1 (for the same reasons as at **e** above). It follows, then, that N + 2 + E = 12 (or N + E = 10). Now, if E must be even (see **d** above), E can only be 4 or 6. The same must be the case for N.

h Since 5 × 5NE = 2820 (line 4) and since N and E can be only 4 or 6, a little trial and error will show that the first equation works only if E is 4 and N is 6.

i B must, then, be 3, to account for T being 2 in the first addition.
   The only other possibility is for B to be 8, but I is 8 (see **f**).
j Working out the third line of the equation shows that A must
   be 9. Q.E.D.

Solution 19 (Puzzle 114)

C is the correct answer. The sequence represents the simplest numeric
series, i.e. 1, 2, 3, 4, 5, 6, 7 . . . The square represents the number
1, the circle 2, and the triangle 5. In addition, the shape representing
the smaller number in any combination of shapes encloses the other
shape(s). C is correct, because its combination of shapes adds up
to 8—the next number in the numeric sequence—*and* because the
shapes representing the smaller numbers enclose those representing
larger numbers. The shapes in D also add to 8, but the circle
(representing 2) encloses the square (representing 1), so breaking the
rule that smaller shapes enclose larger shapes. No other combination
of shapes adds up to 8.

Solution 20 (Puzzle 50)

10 32 54 76 98 (Read from either end.) Answers with a pair beginning
with zero must, of course, be disallowed.

Solution 21 (Puzzle 30)

The contestant can win $305 at the very most. She would need to
draw three notes of each denomination before drawing a fourth $50
note.

Solution 22 (Puzzle 17)

The words SWINDLE and CHAPTER meet the conditions of the
puzzle.

Solution 23 (Puzzle 62)

a Given 2 down, 6 across must end in 6 or 8.

b Only 196, 256, 576 and 676 are three-digit perfect squares (see 6 across) ending in 6 or 8. Since none does, in fact, end in 8, 2 down must end in 6. Therefore 2 down is 246.

c The only squares of odd numbers (see 2 across) beginning with 2 are 225 (= 15^2) and 289 (= 17^2).

d But 2 across cannot end in 9, since 3 down would then be either 975 or 951. Three down cannot be 975, for then 4 across would have digits adding to more than 11. For the same reason, 951 is also out. Therefore 2 across must be 225.

e Consequently, 3 down must be 531.

f Hence 7 across must be 123 if 5 down is to equal 3 and yet 7 across be odd.

g It follows that 4 across must end in 1. Moreover, 4 across must start with either a 1 or a 2 if its digits are to add to 11.

h Consequently 4 down must be 19 or 28 if the sum of its digits is to equal 10. Thus 6 across must end with 86 or 96.

i But from b above, the only possibility for 6 across is 196.

j Hence 4 across is 14231, and 1 down can then only be 1221.

The full solution is, then:

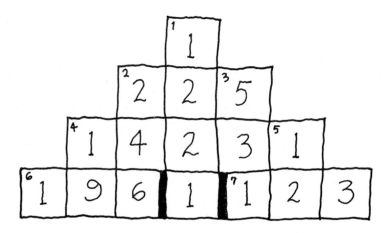

Solution 24 (Puzzle 3)

When the man has walked 3 kilometres, he has reached the top of the hill and immediately turns for home. At this point, his dog has walked only 1.5 kilometres. When the man has walked a further kilometre, the dog has walked an additional 0.5 kilometres. Both man and beast are now 2 kilometres from home. At this pont, the dog turns round and follows his master home, so making its walk 4 kilometres in all.

Solution 25 (Puzzle 34)

Claudette was closest to the correct answer (which was 107). Let R represent the right answer, and assume, first, that R is less than Alice's answer (i.e. less than 89). In that case, one or other of the following equations represents one girl's answer being twice as wrong as another's:

$$2(89 - R) = (105 - R) \quad 2(105 - R) = (111 - R) \quad 2(89 - R) = (111 - R)$$

No equation, however, yields an answer for R that renders any one answer *nine* times as wrong as any other answer. Assume, next, that R is greater than Beatrice's answer (i.e. greater than 111). One or other of the following equations would, then, represent one answer being twice as wrong as another:

$$(R - 105) = 2(R - 111) \quad 2(R - 105) = (R - 89) \quad 2(R - 111) = (R - 89)$$

But, for the same reasons as above, none of these equations yields a suitable value for R. Next, assume that R is between 89 and 105. Similar reasoning will show that the resulting equations do not yield suitable values for R. It is only when we assume that R is between 105 and 111 that a resulting equation yields a value for R that makes one girl twice as wrong as another and a third girl nine times as wrong as another. And that is when R is 107, making Claudette's answer of 105 nearest to the correct answer.

Solution 26 (Puzzle 5)

I am walking twice as fast as the escalator. The length of any journey is equal to the speed at which the journey is undertaken multiplied by the time the journey takes. Now, since the length of the escalator is the same whether I walk up it or down it, we can say that my average speed going up the escalator multiplied by 2 minutes is equal to my average speed going down the escalator multiplied by 6 minutes. But my average speed upwards is just the average speed of my walking (call this W) *plus* the average speed of the escalator (call this E); and my average speed downwards is just the average speed of my walking *minus* the average speed of the escalator. So, in algebraic terms, $2(W + E) = 6(W - E)$, which reduces to $W = 2E$.

Solution 27 (Puzzle 22)

Three sherbert bombs, 9 musk sticks and 3 chocolate bullets. If the lollies are shared equally, Mrs Sweetmum must buy each lolly in multiples of 3. Moreover, because she buys more musk sticks than any other lolly, the minimum number of musk sticks she must buy is 6. Finally, because she spends only 17 cents, the maximum number of musk sticks she can buy while still buying the minimum number (3) of each other lolly is 9. Hence the only possibilities are:

Sherbert bombs	Musk sticks	Bullets	Cost (c)
3	6	3	14
3	9	3	17
6	9	6	23
3	9	6	20

Only the second possibility divests Mrs Sweetmum of exactly 17 cents.

Solution 28 (Puzzle 10)

2^{2^2} (i.e. 2 to the power of 2 to the power of 2).

Solution 29 (Puzzle 27)

One hundred and twenty-five members took the flight. Let F be the undiscounted cost of the fare. Since ¾F was paid by the first 100 members to sign up for the trip (i.e. ¾ of $24 000), then F equals $240. So the discounted fare was $180 (i.e. ¾ of $240), making the early birds' contribution to the total cost of the fares $18 000. The remaining members paid $240 each or $6000. This is equivalent to 25 others taking the flight, making the total number of flyers 125.

Solution 30 (Puzzle 66)

The pool is 100 metres long. When Sam and Thomas first meet, Sam has swum one length plus 10 metres and Thomas one length less 10 metres. So *together* they have swum two lengths of the pool. When next they meet, Sam has swum three lengths of the pool less 80 metres, and Thomas has swum one length plus 80 metres. So *together* they have swum four lengths of the pool *or twice the distance they had travelled when first they met.* Consequently, because each was swimming at a constant rate and without breaks, each had swum twice as far when they met the second time as they had swum when they first met. So, using Sam's relative positions (and Thomas's yield the same result), we can say that:

$$2(L + 10) = (3L - 80)$$

making L, the length of the pool, equal to 100 metres.

Solution 31 (Puzzle 61)

The number can only be 222 666. You would have spurred on your imagination – or saved yourself much arithmetic labour – if you had first established that the third digit in the number must, given the clues, be 2. Knowing that, the answer should really jump out at you!

Solution 32 (Puzzle 18, Part A)

The sequence is continued by the letters PQR. It is composed of two sub-sequences, one ascending the alphabet in regularly increasing leaps (i.e. K, LM, NOP . . .) and the other descending the alphabet in regularly decreasing leaps (i.e. UTS, RQ . . .). With the letters so far given, it should be obvious that the second sub-sequence is next in line, yielding P, which is followed by the next group of letters from the first sub-sequence; namely, QRST. So the next three letters in the whole sequence are PQR.

Solution 33 (Puzzle 108)

Johnny could not have been telling the *whole* truth, for his mother's only cousin's only aunt's only grandchild is Johnny himself; so he either lied when he said "No" or got a little confused when he tried to point out the real culprit.

Solution 34 (Puzzle 59)

In order of distance, the stations on the Great Eastern Railway Line are Lilydale, Ringwood, Box Hill, Camberwell and Belgrave.

a From sentence 2 of the puzzle, Ringwood must precede Camberwell and Box Hill, and both Box Hill and Lilydale must precede Camberwell.

b From sentences 1 and 3, Belgrave must be the most distant station.

c From the last part of sentence 3, it follows that Ringwood cannot be the station closest to Flinders Street.

d From sentence 5, Lilydale must precede Box Hill.

Hence, from **a, c** and **d** together, it follows that Lilydale is the closest station. From **a** and **b**, Ringwood must be the next station, and, from **a**, Box Hill is next on the line. Since, from **b**, Belgrave is the most distant station, Camberwell must lie between Box Hill and Belgrave.

Solution 35 (Puzzle 65)

Graeme sold the article costing $160. You can see this clearly if you add, in ascending order, the commissions available to the two salesmen, i.e. $1, $2, $4, $8, $16, $32, $64, $128 and $256. The total of all bar the last commission is $255, *which is precisely $1 less than the biggest commission.* Since there are no other sub-sets of commissions different by only $1, Graeme — having received $1 less in commissions than Gordon — must have sold all bar the most expensive item.

Solution 36 (Puzzle 1)

Mr Sailor was boating in the Pacific Ocean. His journey appears to have taken 1 day and 4 hours only because he crossed the International Date Line (and a time zone).

Solution 37 (Puzzle 37)
The time is 8.45. If you spent a good deal of time solving this puzzle by trial and error, you overlooked a simple short-cut: namely, adding 2 hours to the average of the times showing on the professor's 4 clocks.

Solution 38 (Puzzle 20)
120 kilometres. The only relevant facts in the puzzle are the fly's speed and the time of the train's journey.

Solution 39 (Puzzle 67, Part A)
The next two letters are V and Y. The letters in the sequence are separated by the next 3, 2, 1 and 0 ascending letters respectively, and this is repeated over and over.

Solution 40 (Puzzle 15)
Whatever the speeds and whatever the actual distances travelled, Sturrock must win the race. If you are a little puzzled by this, prove the result with an example (say, a 50 kilometre race with Sturrock averaging 50 kilometres an hour for the whole trip and Edmonds 48 kilometres an hour for the first half and 52 kilometres an hour for the second half, which would, in fact, see Sturrock the winner by 5.77 seconds).

Solution 41 (Puzzle 70)
To the right of Sachaverell cannot be the ventriloquist (since the ventriloquist is opposite) nor the guitarist (since a woman is to the left of the guitarist). That person must, then, be the oenologist or the critic. But he or she cannot be the oenologist, for then Chloe would be to that person's right — and hence opposite Sachaverell — causing the engaged couple to be sitting, not together, but opposite. Therefore, it is the *critic* who is at Sachaverell's right. Consequently, either the oenologist or the guitarist is sitting to Sachaverell's left. That person cannot, however, be the oenologist, since on the oenologist's right sits Chloe. But Sachaverell is sitting there. Therefore the guitarist is on Sachaverell's left, making Sachaverell the oenologist. Hence Chloe is the critic, since she is to the right of the oenologist. And since a woman sits to the left of the guitarist, that woman — who is also the ventriloquist — can only be Daphne: leaving Algernon as the guitarist.

Solution 42 (Puzzle 63)

Train C (and also A) is travelling twice as fast as B, and A and C should have passed each other in 6 seconds. One way to approach this puzzle is to give the train an arbitrary length, say 240 metres. Consider, then, a passenger on board train B. To her, A appears to be travelling much more slowly than it really is, travelling, seemingly, at A – B metres per second. Since it takes A 24 seconds to overtake B, A – B = 240 metres divided by 24 seconds or 10 metres per second. To that same passenger, C appears to be travelling much faster than it really is, travelling, seemingly, at C + B metres per second or, since the speeds of A and C are the same, at A + B metres per second. Since it takes C 8 seconds to pass B, A + B = 240 metres divided by 8 seconds or 30 metres per second. Since we know from above that A – B = 10 metres per second, it follows from both equations that A = 20 metres per second and B = 10 metres per second. Since A is travelling at the same speed as C, it follows that C is travelling twice as fast as B. Moreover, if A and C are travelling at 20 metres per second, a passenger on one will see the other pass at 40 metres per second, and, being 240 metres long, it should pass in just 6 seconds.

Solution 43 (Puzzle 14)

The philatelist bought 29 stamps, comprising 25 three-cent stamps, 3 five-cent stamps and 1 ten-cent stamp. The answer follows quickly once you realise that to get the most stamps possible, the philatelist must buy as many *three*-cent stamps as possible (while, of course, buying at least one each of the other two stamps).

Solution 44 (Puzzle 24)

Allan scored 93, Brian 39, Chris 31 and David 13. Your work is made much lighter once you realise that since Allan's mark has only two digits, is 80 marks more than another student's mark and is exactly three times another student's mark, it can be one of only 81, 84, 87, 90, 93, 96 or 99.

Solution 45 (Puzzle 2)

No, the answer is not 1500 kilometres an hour, as you might expect. If the second 500 kilometres of the journey were at a speed of 1500 kilometres an hour, it would take the plane a mere 20 minutes. This, together with the 1 hour it took for the first 500 kilometres, would make the whole 1000 kilometre journey take one and a third hours: and that works out at an average speed of 750 kilometres an hour, not the required 1000 kilometres an hour. The correct answer is that it is *impossible* for the aircraft to average 1000 kilometres an hour. A little arithmetic will bear this out. Let x be the number of hours it takes to travel the last 500 kilometres. Then:

$$\frac{1000 \text{ km}}{1 + x \text{ hours}} = 1000 \text{ km/h}$$

For this equation to be true, x must equal 0. In other words, the plane would need to fly the last 500 kilometres *in no time at all*. Since this is impossible, the aircraft simply cannot achieve an average speed of 1000 kilometres an hour, given the conditions set in the puzzle.

Solution 46 (Puzzle 74)

The trick in this puzzle is to realise that Thomas must have been born on 29 February and so has a birthday only every 4 years. Only then is it possible for Odette to have, at any time in her life, 5 times as many birthdays as her brother. And that would happen when Odette turned 25.

Solution 47 (Puzzle 116)

Mr Greatcharm's new bride is 30 years old. The clues yield the following formula:

$$W + 3 = \frac{1}{3}(69 + W)$$

where W is the wife's age, 3 is the number of Greatcharm's previous wives, and 69 is Greatcharm's current age.

Solution 48 (Puzzle 49)
The man had $5000 left for his grandchildren. The clues yield the
following formula:

$$\$50\,000 = M + \$10\,000 + \tfrac{1}{3}(\$50\,000 - M)$$

where M is the money the son got on reaching his majority, being,
in fact, $35 000. So the son's two gifts add to $45 000, leaving $5000
of the original $50 000 for the man's grandchildren.

Solution 49 (Puzzle 75)
The two numbers are 3649 and 7298. Logic could have provided
you with the answer rather than trial and error:

a One number must start with 3, since 3 is the first number listed.
b The other number, then, can only start with a 6 or a 7.
c 8 must end one of the numbers, since it is the last number listed.
d Because the only 6 must be either the first or the second digit
   in a number, the 8 must end the bigger of the two numbers. Hence
   9 must end the smaller number.
e If 6 begins the bigger number, then the 7 cannot follow the 3
   but must follow the 6.
f Suppose, then, that the 6 does begin the bigger number. We then
   have:

$$3\;?\;?\;9 \quad \text{and} \quad 6\;7\;?\;8$$

with 4, 9 and 2 the only numbers not yet allocated. But if we
substitute each of these unallocated digits in turn into the larger
number and then divide by 2, we get, in all cases, a number
possessing digits other than just the three we have to allocate.
g Hence 7 begins the bigger number. It follows that the second digit
   of the smaller number must be 6. We then have:

$$3\;6\;?\;9 \quad \text{and} \quad 7\;?\;?\;8$$

with 4, 9 and 2, again, the only numbers not yet allocated. If
we substitute these digits in turn into the smaller number and
then multiply by 2, we find that the 4 alone yields a result that
uses only the numbers allowed. So the smaller number is 3649
and the bigger is 7298.

Solution 50 (Puzzle 40)

Poxyalic-10 and Symochlorine were alkaline, Ethylate was neither acidic nor alkaline, and the remaining three were acidic. The clues can be abbreviated like this.

a Pox = Sym
b Dr = Gl
c Dr < > Eth
d Sym < > Tr
e Pox < > Eth

First, by **a** and given that only one compound is neither acidic nor alkaline, it follows that Pox cannot be that compound. Suppose, then, that Pox is acidic. Then, by **a** and **d**, Tr is not acidic, and, by **e**, neither is Eth. Since there are only 3 acidic compounds, by **c**, neither Dr nor Gl can be acidic. But this makes 4 compounds out of 6 that are not acidic, yet we are told that 3 compounds are acidic.

Consequently, Pox must be alkaline, and, by **a**, so too is Sym. Since we are told that there is only one neutral compound and 2 alkaline compounds, it follows from **b** that Dr and Gl are acidic. Moreover, by **c** and the fact that the 2 alkaline compounds have already been accounted for, it follows that Eth must be neutral. This leaves Tr as the remaining acidic compound.

Solution 51 (Puzzle 23)

Mr Amneez is 40. Let the girls' ages be represented as x, $x + 5$ and $x + 10$. We are told that $\frac{1}{2}(x + 10) = x$, which yields 10 as the age of the youngest daughter. The oldest daughter is, then, 20, and since she was born when Amneez was himself 20, he must now be 40.

Solution 52 (Puzzle 124, Part A)

92 is the odd number out. All the others are divisible by 3 (and so too is the sum of their individual digits).

Solution 53 (Puzzle 101)

Bruce made a profit of $3, Allan a profit of $2.20, David a loss of $2.20 and Colin a loss of $3. Because each player began with $7 in the form of 35 coins, the first clue can be expressed as:

a $A + B + C + D = 140$

The remaining three clues can be expressed similarly:

b $A + D = B + C$
c $A = C + D + 2$
d $B + D = A + C + 8.$

From **c**, we get $C + D = A - 2$, which, when substituted into **a**, yields:

e $2A + B = 142.$

From **b**, we get $D = B + C - A$, which, when substituted into **d**, yields:

f $2B - 2A = 8.$

Solving **e** and **f** together yields $A = 46$ and $B = 50$. Substituting A into **c** yields:

g $C + D = 40$

and substituting A and B into **d** yields:

h $D - C = 4.$

Solving **g** and **h** together yields $C = 20$ and $D = 24$. Expressed in dollars, we get $A = 9.20, $B = 10, $C = 4, and $D = 4.80 as the money each player had left after the game.

Solution 54 (Puzzle 115)

The message reads:
"The vowels in this message are represented by numbers and the consonants have been replaced by the next letter in the alphabet."

Solution 55 (Puzzle 8)

The groceries were priced at $1.57 and 57 cents. Let x be the price of the cheaper sort. Then (1 + x) will be the price of the other sort. With just 7 items bought for $9.99, the only possibilities are:

$$x + 6(1 + x) = 9.99 \qquad 2x + 5(1 + x) = 9.99$$
$$3x + 4(1 + x) = 9.99 \qquad 4x + 3(1 + x) = 9.99$$
$$5x + 2(1 + x) = 9.99 \qquad 6x + (1 + x) = 9.99$$

Now, because Joe never offers a discount for multiple purchases, his prices must be set at no more than 2 decimal places. (A price of $1.637, for example, could not apply to a single purchase expressed in standard decimal currency.) A little experimentation will show that only the first equation yields an answer for x that has no more than 2 decimal places, i.e. 0.57.

Solution 56 (Puzzle 71)

India came first in the competition, with Australia second, West Indies third, England fourth and Pakistan fifth. Hence Richie Wrongun came closest to predicting the result.

One way to solve this puzzle is to take any one prediction and assume it is correct, rule out the chosen commentator's two other predictions, and then consider the effect on the other commentators' predictions. If your assumption leads to a commentator being wrong in each of his three predictions, or to a team being placed in more than one position, then your assumption must be rejected. You should then assume that some other prediction is correct and repeat the process. Eventually you will hit upon the one set of predictions that does not yield a contradiction. For example, given Clive Stumping's prediction that the West Indies came first, Richie Wrongun's predictions that Australia came first and the West Indies second must both be wrong, so making his prediction that England came fourth true. Krishnan Murti's predictions that India came first and the West Indies fifth must also be rejected, making his prediction that England came second true. But this conflicts with our earlier result that England came fourth. Hence, the assumption that the West Indies came first must be abandoned and another made.

Once you have worked out the result of the competition, give each commentator points equivalent to the number of places by which each of his predictions was out, and then total the points. The commentator with the fewest points was the best predictor.

Solution 57 (Puzzle 93)

The explorer made 7 treks to cross the desert. Consider the following representation of the desert:

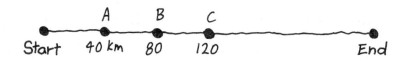

Trek 1: With 4 days' rations, he travels to A, stores 2 days' rations and then returns to the start. Time = 2 days.
Trek 2: Travels to B, picking up one day's rations stored at A, stores a day's rations at B and then returns to the start. Time = 4 days.
Trek 3: Same as for trek 2. Point B now has two days' rations. Time = 4 days.
Trek 4: Same as for trek 1. Time = 2 days.
Trek 5: Travels to C, picking up a day's rations at A and a day's rations at B. He leaves a day's rations at C before returning to the start, picking up a needed day's rations at A on the way. Time = 6 days.
Trek 6: Travels to A, stores a day's rations, and then returns to the start. Time = 2 days.
Trek 7: Sets off across the desert with 4 days' rations, picking up a day's rations at A, at B and at C. Time = 7 days.
Total time = 27 days.

Solution 58 (Puzzle 35)

The secretary had won 10 matches and the treasurer 9 matches. Since a player's percentage is the number of matches won divided by the number of matches played multiplied by 100, it follows that the number of matches won is equal to the number of matches played multiplied by the player's percentage divided by 100. Now, given the number of matches the secretary won, it follows that at least 10 matches had been played in the season. So start at 10 and work your way to 21, each time multiplying this number (the number of matches played) by the treasurer's percentage expressed as a decimal (i.e. 0.8181). What you are looking for is a result that is more or less a whole number (since the number of matches played must be a whole number). And this occurs only when the number of matches is 11 (the result being 8.9991). So the treasurer must have won 9 matches out of 11 played.

Solution 59 (Puzzle 76)
The two muddled words are SECRET and EXPOSED.

Solution 60 (Puzzle 7)
7 ingots
a Place 3 ingots in each tray of the scales. If the scales are in balance, the ingot not on the scales is the heavier one.
b If, instead, one tray is heavier, discard the 3 ingots from the lighter tray and put one of the ingots from the heavier tray to one side. Put the remaining 2 ingots in opposite trays of the scales. If the scales are in balance, the ingot put to one side is the heavier one. If the scales are not in balance, the ingot in the heavier tray is, obviously, the heavier one.

8 ingots
a Place 3 ingots in each tray of the scales. If the scales are in balance, one of the 2 ingots not being weighed is the heavier one. Clear the scales and weigh these 2 ingots alone to see which one is heavier.
b If, instead, one tray of 3 ingots is heavier than the other, follow the steps in b above to find the heavier ingot.

Solution 61 (Puzzle 81)
The family had 16 children: 5 boys and 11 girls. Let T = the total number of children, B = the total number of boys, and G = the total number of girls. It follows that $(B - 1)$ = the number of brothers each boy has; $(G - 1)$ = the number of sisters each girl has; and $T = B + G$. The clues can be expressed algebraically as follows:

$$(B - 1) = \tfrac{1}{4}(B + G) \text{ and } (G - 1) = 2B$$

which, when solved simultaneously, yield $B = 5$ and $G = 11$.

Solution 62 (Puzzle 64)
Paul could have written something like this:
"Paul Bloom will be expelled from this school."
If the sentence is wrong, then Paul would be expelled from the school, thus making the sentence, not wrong, but right! And if it is right, Paul would not be expelled from the school, so making the sentence wrong, not right! This is the cause of the teacher's bafflement.

Solution 63 (Puzzle 94)

Paul and Donald drive Fords, while John and Chris drive Holdens. Because John and Chris drive the same make of car, and since Chris drives a Holden if Paul does, it follows that if Paul drives a Holden, John does too. But John and Paul drive different cars. Therefore Paul cannot drive a Holden but drives, instead, a Ford. So John must drive a Holden, and so too does Chris. Finally, Donald does not drive a Holden if Paul drives a Ford; so Donald must drive a Ford too.

Solution 64 (Puzzle 25, Part A)

7 and J continue the sequence. The embedded numbers form a sequence of their own, being –2 followed by a multiplication by 3 each time. The number of letters *between* the letters increases by 1 each time.

Solution 65 (Puzzle 97)

Jim's profit was $1.50. He tendered $1 and got back $2 in change. His profit so far is $1. But he also got a chocolate bar valued at 50 cents. So his total profit is $1.50.

Solution 66 (Puzzle 45)

The aviary had 1200 birds. Let P = the original number of pens, and T = the total number of birds. The two clues can then be expressed as $\frac{T}{30}$ = P and $\frac{T}{40}$ = (P − 10), which yield 1200 as the value for T.

David□

Solution 67 (Puzzle 104)

The clock will show the correct time on 11 occasions in the next 12 hours, at approximately 1.05, 2.11, 3.16, 4.22, 5.27, 6.33, 7.38, 8.44, 9.49, 10.55 and 12.00.

Solution 68 (Puzzle 68)

The course of the disease is: fever, coughing, hallucinations, rash, coughing and rash. Let the symptoms be abbreviated to R, F, C and H and the days be represented as 1 to 6. Now if 2 is C, 3 cannot be C (since a symptom lasts only one day at a time), nor, given the clues, can it be F. Nor can 3 be R, since 4 is R. Therefore, 3 must be H. If 4 is R, 5 cannot be R, nor, by the clues, is it F or H. Hence 5 can only be C. If 5 is C, 6 cannot be C, nor, given the clues, can it be F or H. So 6 must be R. This leaves only day 1, and since F is the only symptom not yet allocated, 1 must be F.

Solution 69 (Puzzle 36)

Since Alice and Springs had 20 litres of water between them before meeting the third explorer, they would have had only 6⅔ litres each after sharing it with him. Consequently, Alice gave up 5⅓ litres of his water (since he originally had 12 litres) and Springs gave up 1⅓ litres of his (since he had 8 litres). That means that Alice gave up four times as much water as Springs and so should get four times as many slices of beef as Springs. Algebraically, 4S + S = 20, making S (the number of slices Springs should get) equal to 4.

Solution 70 (Puzzle 120)

The sentence was: "A verb is a word representing action."

You should have got a start knowing that the sentence was concerned with grammar.

Solution 71 (Puzzle 46)

Since the lecturer had a double doctorate, but both Stewart and Charles had just a standard university education, the lecturer must be Campbell. Moreover, since Stewart beat the lawyer, he must be the surgeon, leaving Campbell as the lawyer.

Solution 72 (Puzzle 33)

I am 42 years old. The clues should have saved you the tedium of solving this puzzle solely by trial and error. For a start, my brother must be at least in his thirties if my age is to have at least two digits in it and he is 25 years older than I am. A little mental arithmetic should then show that if he is in his thirties, I could only be 12 (given that the digits of my age added together equal the first digit of his age and that he is 25 years older than I am). Suppose, though, that he is in his forties. Similarly, I would have to be 22. Likewise, if he is in his fifties, I would have to be 32; if he's in his sixties, I would have to be 42; and so on up to his nineties, in which case I would have to be 72. In each case, the last digit of my age is 2. Consequently, the last digit of his age must be 7. And now it should be easy to see that the only instance where the digits of his age, when multiplied together, equal my age is when he is 67 and I am 42.

Solution 73 (Puzzle 73)

Susan is the mother, Peter the father, Colin the son and Anne the daughter. Being *natural* children, it is impossible for a child to be older than a parent. Hence, once it is established—as the only consistent possibility—that Peter is older than Colin and Susan older than Anne, the family relationships are easily inferred.

Solution 74 (Puzzle 89)

The answer is: 12 + 34 + 5 + 6 + 78 + 9. This comes to 144, which is the square of 12. The other likely candidate is 123 squared (or 15 129), but no addition of the given numbers, however grouped, will yield 15 129.

Solution 75 (Puzzle 83)

Only switches 5, 3, 2, 4, 5 and 3, thrown in that order will produce the desired result. A combination of more than 6 switches will, in certain cases, produce the same mixture, but any such combination would fail the requirement of producing the mixture in the shortest possible time.

Solution 76 (Puzzle 95)

Sir James Blueblood is the director of the public company, Mr Bluechip is the Queen's Counsel, Mr Silverspoon is the orthopaedic surgeon, and Mr Risingstar is the stockbroker. From the clues, we see that the Queen's Counsel paid twice as much tax as the director, the surgeon twice as much as the Queen's Counsel, and the stockbroker twice as much again. That is, each man's tax burden increased by a factor of 2, with the director paying the least tax. Now, since they all paid exact dollars, and because the "knighted member" (Sir James Blueblood) paid an *odd* amount of tax ($2731), it follows that he must have paid the least tax. So Sir James is the company director. Now Silverspoon could brag to only *one* of his friends, so he must have paid the second highest amount of tax, making him the surgeon. Bluechip paid half as much as Silverspoon, so he must be the Queen's Counsel, which leaves Risingstar as the heavily taxed stockbroker.

Solution 77 (Puzzle 72, Part A)

The number 17 should read 19. The series progresses by adding ascending multiples of 4, beginning with 4 (i.e. by adding 4, 8, 12, 16, 20, 24 and so on).

Solution 78 (Puzzle 106)

The three clues given can be expressed this way:

a C + A are lighter than M + D.
b A + D are heavier than M + C.
c A + M are equal to C + D.

From **b** and **c** together, it follows that D is heavier than M. From **a** and **c** together, it follows that M is heavier than C. Therefore D is also heavier than C, since D is heavier than M. Suppose, now, that A were heavier than D. For **c** to be true, it would have to be the case that M is lighter than C. But M is heavier than C. Nor do A and D weigh the same, for then, by **c**, M and C would weigh the same, which they do not. So D is heavier than A, and, being heavier than M and C also, it follows that D(arren) is the heaviest jockey. Moreover, if Darren is the heaviest, it follows from **c** that Clive is the lightest.

Solution 79 (Puzzle 111)

Humphreys is the culprit. The clues can be set out like this:

Detainee	1st claim	2nd claim
S	Not-S	D
H	Not-H	Not-S
D	Not-D	Not-H

All you need do is treat each claim in turn as if it were true and its partner false, and note the effect on the other claims made. You will find that only when the claim "Not-H" is false is the whole set of claims free from internal contradiction. (For example, if Humphreys's first claim is true, his second is false. Consequently, Simpkins's first claim is false and his second true. But this is a contradiction, saying, in effect, that *both* Simpkins and Dagge committed the robbery.)

Solution 80 (Puzzle 11)

10 (December). On the next day the invaders would, though, be back across the border, but nonetheless fighting a losing battle.

Solution 81 (Puzzle 9)

$11.25. The causes of the reductions are independent of each other. The first reduction makes her bill $15, and a further 25% off this leaves $11.25.

Solution 82 (Puzzle 78)

The three hoses together should fill the pool in just 6 minutes. Consider how full the pool would be after 1 minute. The first hose would have contributed one-thirtieth of the pool's capacity, the second hose one-twentieth, and the third one-twelfth. So together they would have supplied $\frac{1}{30} + \frac{1}{20} + \frac{1}{12}$ or one-sixth of the pool's capacity. Obviously, in a further 5 minutes (making 6 minutes in all), the pool would be full.

Solution 83 (Puzzle 82)

The temptation must be avoided to answer 16 kilometres an hour (16 being the average of 20 and 12); for the correct answer is, in fact, 15 kilometres an hour! Try the calculation using, say, 20 kilometres as the length of each leg, to verify this admittedly surprising answer.

Solution 84 (Puzzle 39)

Saturday. One way of solving this puzzle is to work backwards:

a Five days after Tuesday = Sunday.
b Tomorrow week = the same day (but not the same date) as tomorrow.
c The day preceding tomorrow = today.
d The day after c = tomorrow.

That is, tomorrow is Sunday; hence today is Saturday.

Solution 85 (Puzzle 91)

20 cents. The rail-motor is a sixth slower than the first train, for which I am charged $1.20. To see that the rail-motor is a sixth slower, try solving the following equations based on the clues given: $T = \frac{3}{4}D/A$, and $2T = \frac{1}{4}D/B$, where T is the time taken for the first leg of the journey, D is the distance of the whole journey, A is the speed of the first train and B the speed of the second. The result is $6B = A$.

Solution 86 (Puzzle 12)

Mrs Childlover will be 36. For most puzzles of this sort, there are mathematical short-cuts to the faithful but often tedious trial-and-error method. In this puzzle, you could start by noticing that from the birth of the third child (when Mrs Childlover was 25), the sum of her children's ages will start at 3 and increase by 3 each year. That is, the sums will be 3, 6, 9, 12, 15 and so on, according to the formula $3 + 3n$ (where n is the number of *subsequent* years). Now, at some time in the future, Mrs Childlover's age will be the same as one of those sums. At that time, the equation $25 + n = 3 + 3n$ will be true. This reduces to $n = 11$. Therefore, in 11 years' time—when Mrs Childlover is 36—her age will be the same as the sum of her children's ages.

Solution 87 (Puzzle 77)

The answer is 6 seconds and not, as you might imagine, 4 seconds. Start counting from the *fall* of the first drop, and add 2 seconds for each additional drop.

Solution 88 (Puzzle 113)

Frank (with 3 tricks) partnered Iain (with 5 tricks), and lost to Graeme (with 10 tricks) and his partner, John (who won 8 tricks). One needs to establish, first of all, who partnered whom. Now, Frank could not have partnered Graeme, for then John would have won 5 tricks more than Frank, and Graeme only 2 tricks more than Frank. This would give John more tricks than Graeme, and yet Graeme won the most tricks. Suppose, then, that Iain partnered Graeme. John would then have won 5 tricks more than Iain and Iain half as many tricks as John. This is possible only if John had won 10 tricks and Iain 5. Frank, with 2 tricks fewer than his partner, would then have won 8 tricks, leaving, out of a possible 26 tricks, only 3 for Graeme. But Graeme won the most tricks. Hence John must have partnered Graeme, leaving Frank to partner Iain. We can now say that:

a $F = I - 2$
b $J = F + 5$ or, from a, $J = I + 3$
c $G = 21$
d $F + G + J + I = 26$.

Substituting a, b and c into d yields $I = 5$, from which it follows that $F = 3$, $G = 10$, and $J = 8$.

Solution 89 (Puzzle 19)

The plane has been flying over the north pole.

Solution 90 (Puzzle 90)

Say the quantity of secretarial work done is 60 units. (It doesn't matter which amount you use here.) Then $6W + 3T$ will produce 15 units of work in a day, while $4W + 4T$ will produce 12 units of work in a day. Solving these equations simultaneously produces the results $W = 2$ and $T = 1$, showing that the word processor is twice as productive as the typewriter.

Solution 91 (Puzzle 13)

The correct time is 7.30 p.m. You can substantially cut down the number of possibilities you need to check by realising that the magnitudes of the greatest advance (10 minutes an hour) and the greatest retardation (12 minutes an hour) indicate that the correct time must lie *between* the two times noted by the Professor.

Solution 92 (Puzzle 98)

If 7 teachers have only a bachelor's degree, 43 must have postgraduate degrees (i.e. a master's and/or a doctorate). Now, 24 teachers have a master's degree and 20 have a doctorate, making a total of 44 teachers if none had *both* postgraduate degrees. But since there are only 43 teachers with postgraduate degrees, it follows that 1 teacher must have both a master's and a doctorate.

Solution 93 (Puzzle 107)

There will always be the same number of black balls in the first bag as red balls in the second, regardless of how many black balls you happen to transfer from the second to the first bag. Perhaps the best way to see this is by means of an example. If you removed 3 red and 9 black balls from the second bag and placed them in the first bag, there will be 9 black balls in the first bag. But by taking only 3 red balls across, you've left 9 red balls behind in the second bag!

Solution 94 (Puzzle 69)

There are two solutions to this puzzle, both closely related:

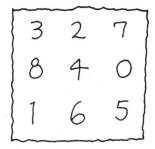
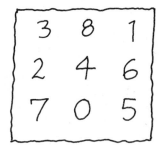

Solution 95 (Puzzle 79)

The temptation must be resisted to argue that since 10.00 to 10.00 is 12 hours, and since the clock is losing 10 minutes an hour, then it will be 120 minutes, or two hours behind, when *the clock* next reads 10.00. The clock will be 2 hours behind when *12 real* hours have passed, but when 12 *clock* hours have passed, it will be more than 2 hours behind. It will, in fact, be 2 hours and 24 minutes behind. So the real time in 12 *clock* hours' time is 12.24.

Solution 96 (Puzzle 102)

Adam plays rugby and tennis, James plays cricket and football, and Charles plays baseball and soccer. The clues tell you that:

a Charles is not the cricketer (since he and the cricketer work together);

b Adam despises baseball, so we can assume that he doesn't play it;

c Adam is neither the cricketer nor the soccer player (since those three share the driving to work); and

d Charles is neither the footballer nor the tennis player (since these three went to the same school).

We can deduce, now, that Adam plays two of football, rugby and tennis, and Charles plays two of baseball, soccer and rugby. Now, Adam cannot play both football and tennis, since we are told that the footballer does not play tennis. Suppose, instead, that he plays football and rugby. If Adam plays rugby, Charles doesn't, which leaves Charles with baseball and soccer as his two sports. The two remaining sports—which James would play—are cricket and tennis. But we are also told that the cricketer is not the tennis player. So Adam cannot play both football and rugby. The one remaining possibility for Adam is that he plays rugby and tennis. Again, it follows that Charles plays baseball and soccer, with the two remaining sports—cricket and football—being played by James.

Solution 97 (Puzzle 112)

The correct time is 1.57. Again there are quicker methods of solving this sort of puzzle than trial and error. For a start, we know that the correct time is neither earlier than 1.50 nor later than 2.16 (for then the clocks would be all fast, or all slow, respectively, which they are not). So the correct time is either between 1.50 and 2.10, or between 2.10 and 2.16. In the following diagram, the correct time is either A or B:

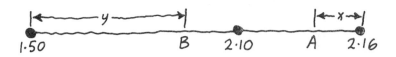

For the average error to be 13 minutes, the sum of all the errors must be 39 minutes (since there are 3 clocks). So, if the correct time is represented by A, it follows that $x + (6 - x) + (26 - x) = 39$, making $x = -7$. But x cannot equal -7 if A is to lie *between* 2.10

and 2.16. So A cannot represent the correct time. Hence B represents the correct time, and it follows that y + (20 – y) + (26 – y) = 39, making y = 7. In other words, B = 1.57.

Solution 98 (Puzzle 85)

Wooster started with the brandy and continued anti-clockwise. (Starting with the tequila and continuing clockwise would also have made Bertie famous, but he may, then, have suffered his feared "digestive catastrophe".) Probably the easiest way to solve this puzzle is to work it backwards; that is, start with the Cointreau and keep counting 9 drinks in one particular direction until you are left with just one drink. Then start with that drink and work forwards; that is, count 9 drinks in the opposite direction. If you find that the whisky would be drunk before the Lillet, go back to the start, and this time work backwards from the Cointreau in the other direction. The drink you are left with that passes the Lillet-before-whisky test is the drink Wooster started with.

Solution 99 (Puzzle 6)

The Colonel's second message was "REINFORCEMENTS NEEDED". The secret of the code is to substitute the letters of the alphabet in reverse, so that A = Z, B = Y and so on. McMuddle-chump's third message, "VOWELS REVERSED LAST MESSAGE", adds to the burden of decryption by asking Headquarters to read the vowels backwards, too, so that A E I O U are to be decrypted as U O I E A respectively.

Solution 100 (Puzzle 31)

Laughlin is the doctor, Crowthers the barrister, Chomley the teacher and Rawlins the dentist. In the order they are given, the clues tell us that:

a neither Laughlin nor Chomley is the barrister (since both were jurors at one of the barrister's trials);

b Crowthers is neither the teacher nor the dentist (since he *and* the teacher go to the dentist in question for treatment);

c Laughlin is not the dentist (since the dentist gives him a discount); and

d neither Laughlin nor Rawlins is the teacher (since they were, at one stage, his pupils).

From this, we know that Chomley must be the teacher. This leaves Rawlins as the dentist, Crowthers as the only one who could be the barrister, and so Laughlin must be the doctor.

Solution 101 (Puzzle 92)

a Because of the result of the second addition (i.e. B + L = B), L must be 0.

b If L = 0, then C multiplied by K must end in 0. Hence C or K must be a 5.

c But C cannot be 5, for then E would have to be 1, to account for a three-digit number as the result of the second multiplication. And then C multiplied by E (plus any carry-over) would be 5 or higher (being, in fact, M). Now, M + C has no carry-over (see the fourth addition). But if C is 5 and M is 5 or greater, there would be a carry-over when M and C are added. Hence C cannot be 5. So, by **b** above, K must be 5.

d If K is 5, then B can only be 1, 3, 7 or 9, to account for the first figure of the first multiplication. A little experimentation will show that neither multiplication will work unless B is 7.

e If B = 7, then, from the first multiplication, C must be 2 (since B = C + K).

f It follows that E must be 3 if the answer to the first multiplication is to be 2275 (which, as we've now discovered, it must).

g This reveals both factors and allows the teacher, by working through the full multiplication, to see that M must be 6 and F must be 8. The full multiplication is, then:

$$
\begin{array}{r}
3\ 2\ 5 \\
2\ 7 \\
\hline
2\ 2\ 7\ 5 \\
6\ 5\ 0\ \\
\hline
8\ 7\ 7\ 5 \\
\end{array}
$$

Solution 102 (Puzzle 110)
One centimetre. The clues that enable you to rank the strings according to length can be expressed this way:

a A + B is shorter than D.
b B + D is longer than A + C.
c B + D is shorter than D + C.
d A + D = B + C.

From **a**, it follows that D is longer than both A and B. From **c**, it follows that C is longer than B. From **b** and **d** together, it follows that B is longer than A. In other words, A is the shortest string. But if that's the case, it follows from **d** that D is longer than C. So the strings must be ranked D, C, B and A in descending order of length. Now, the clues also tell us that B = A + 1 cm. If we substitute this equation into **d**, we get D = C + 1 cm; that is, the longest string is 1 centimetre longer than the second longest string.

Solution 103 (Puzzle 38)
The plane was 18 minutes late. Let A equal the average speed of the plane, W equal the average speed of the wind during both flights, and L equal the distance between Melbourne and Sydney. Now, the average speed of any object is the distance the object travels divided by the time taken to traverse that distance. Hence the following equations apply to the plane's outward-bound, and return, trips respectively:

$$A + W = \frac{L}{1 \text{ hour}}$$
$$A - W = \frac{L}{1.5 \text{ hours}}$$

Solving these equations yields $A = \frac{5}{6}L$ (i.e. given the times for both trips, the plane's absolute speed was five-sixths of the distance between Melbourne and Sydney, whatever that distance may be). Now, the time a journey takes is equal to the distance divided by the average speed for the journey. Since the airline's schedulers are concerned only with an aircraft's actual or absolute speed, the scheduled time for the trip between Melbourne and Sydney – and Sydney and Melbourne – must be L divided by $\frac{5}{6}L$. This reduces to $\frac{6}{5}$ hours or 1 hour and 12 minutes. So, if the plane left Sydney on time at 9.15, its scheduled arrival time in Melbourne must have been 10.27. So, by arriving at 10.45, it arrived 18 minutes late.

Solution 104 (Puzzle 47)

TIMETABLE is the odd word out. All the other words refer to things that *move us* in one way or another.

Solution 105 (Puzzle 117)

The fourth child should pay 16 cents. Probably the best approach to solving this puzzle is to think of all the lollies so far bought as being in the one bag. There would be, in that bag, 6 of each variety of lolly. The cost of this many lollies is the sum of the amounts paid by the first 3 children, i.e. 48 cents. Since the fourth child wants just 2 of each variety of lolly, he should expect to pay one-third of the cost of the imaginary bag of sweets, i.e. 16 cents.

Solution 106 (Puzzle 84)

The cream paint was of satin finish and priced at $3.90, the beige was of matt finish and priced at $1.95, and the white of gloss finish and priced at 65 cents. Since the price of the cream paint is twice the price of the beige, and the price of the beige is three times the price of the white, it follows that white is the cheapest paint and that the cream paint is six times the price of it. Moreover, because the satin paint is $1.95 more than the matt, the satin paint cannot be the cheapest (i.e. cannot be the white) nor the matt paint the dearest (i.e. the cream). This leaves us with just three possibilities:

	Cream	Beige	White
1	Gloss	Satin	Matt
2	Satin	Gloss	Matt
3	Satin	Matt	Gloss

Consider the first possibility. Since the beige paint is three times the price of the white, and since the satin (i.e. beige) is $1.95 more than the matt (i.e. white), it follows that $3W = W + \$1.95$. This yields $0.975 as the price of the white paint. Given standard decimal currency, no one could pay 97½ cents for anything, and since no multiple-purchase discounts are allowed, which might make fractions of cents part of an article's price, this possibility must be ruled out.

Consider, then, the second possibility. Since the cream is six times the price of the white paint, and since the satin (i.e. cream) is $1.95 more than the matt (i.e. white), it follows that $6W = W + \$1.95$. This gives 39 cents as the price of the white paint. Such a price, however, is disallowed by one of Crankety's provisos.

This leaves the third possibility, where the cream paint (i.e. satin) is six times the price of the white paint and three times the price of the beige (i.e. matt) paint, which is itself three times the price of the white. That is, $6W = 3W + \$1.95$. This yields 65 cents as the price of the white gloss paint, \$1.95 as the price of the beige matt paint, and \$3.90 as the price of the cream satin paint. All conditions in the puzzle are now met.

Solution 107 (Puzzle 118)

a First, turn both glasses over. In 5 minutes, when the smaller glass runs out, turn it over again.

b In a further 4 minutes, the bigger glass will have emptied, at which time the smaller glass will have a minute's sand left in its upper bowl. Turn the bigger glass over again.

c When the smaller glass has emptied – in 1 minute's time – there will be a minute's sand in the lower bowl of the bigger glass. Upturn the bigger glass, and in a minute – a total of 11 minutes since you began – the upper bowl of the bigger glass will have emptied.

Solution 108 (Puzzle 99)

He has 4 boys and 7 girls. Let B = the number of boys and G = the number of girls. Then:

$B + G = 11$, and $\tfrac{1}{2}B + G = 9$ (i.e. half a dollar multiplied by the number of boys plus a dollar multiplied by the number of girls equals 9).

These equations resolve to $B = 4$ and $G = 7$.

Solution 109 (Puzzle 42)

25 kilometres. Let x be the distance Tom has travelled between the time he called his mother and the time she catches up to him. His mother has travelled $10 + x$ kilometres in that time. By the time he gets to the airport, Tom has travelled $x + 5$ kilometres since he called his mother, and she has travelled $10 + 2x$ kilometres. Since the speeds of the two vehicles are constant over their respective journeys, the ratios of the distances travelled must be the same. That is, $x/10 + x = x + 5/10 + 2x$. This yields 10 as the only positive answer for x. Therefore, the airport is $10 + 10 + 5$ kilometres from Tom's mother's house.

Solution 110 (Puzzle 88)

Australia drew with England and India, New Zealand defeated Australia and England, England defeated India, and India defeated New Zealand. You can get a grip on this puzzle by noting that only 6 matches can be played between the 4 teams, and so 60 points are to be awarded in all. The clues tell you that New Zealand got 20 points, and a little mental arithmetic will tell you that if New Zealand was *outright* winner and Australia *outright* loser, Australia must have scored only 10 points, and the other two teams 15 points each. Next question: Did Australia win a game for its 10 points, or did it feature in two draws? Suppose that Australia defeated England. Then India must have defeated Australia if Australia's overall tally was just 10 points. This would take India's tally to 20 (since India defeated New Zealand). But India scored only 15. Suppose, next, that Australia defeated India. Then England must have defeated Australia, and also drawn with India. All results are now settled, but there is only one draw, not two as required. So Australia must have drawn its games against England and India. This leaves only the England *v.* India match to settle, which must have gone to England if both teams are to end the competition with 15 points each.

Solution 111 (Puzzle 103)

Solution 112 (Puzzle 57)

The missing number from the third view of the cube is 2. In view 2, the cube has merely been stood on the face opposite the 1, so making the two unseen vertical faces the 2 and the 6 seen in view 1. Now, if the unseen face opposite the 5 were the 6, then the exposed right-hand vertical face in view 2 would have to be the 2 and not the 3. So the face opposite the 5 cannot be the 6. It must, then, be the 2. Now, in view 3, the cube has merely been rotated one face clockwise while sitting on the same face. Consequently, the unknown face must be the one opposite the 5, which, as we've just seen, is the 2.

Solution 113 (Puzzle 86)

The required sequence of switches is:

$$3 \sim 4 \sim 3 \sim 4 \sim 3 \sim 4 \sim 3$$

Solution 114 (Puzzle 96)

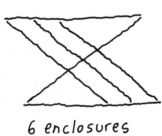

6 enclosures

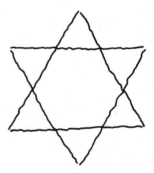

7 enclosures

Solution 115 (Puzzle 4)

Pauline is studying physics and is the archer, Colleen is studying arts and rows for her college, Irene is training to be a doctor and is the cricketer, and Eileen is the engineering student and swims for her college. You can get a start on this puzzle by realising that Pauline and the medical student — by sharing a room — must be either the arts student and the swimmer, or the archer and Irene (since the arts student and the swimmer are in a different college from Irene and the archer). The first possibility is out, because it makes the medical student — who is only just learning to swim — represent her college as a swimmer! Hence Eileen and Colleen are in the same college. Since Eileen is in the same college as the rower, it follows that Colleen is the rower. It also follows that Eileen is the swimmer and Colleen the arts student (since the swimmer and the arts student live in a different college from Irene and the archer). Moreover, Irene must be the cricketer, since cricket is now the only sport not allocated. Finally, since Colleen and the engineering student have adjoining rooms, they must be in the same college, making Eileen the engineering student. This leaves Pauline as the potential physicist.

Solution 116 (Puzzle 109)

a Since D × BK = BK, D must be 1.

b Note that H − C = C. The only possibilities for H and C are 4 and 2, 6 and 3, 8 and 4, and 0 and 5.

c Note that K × C ends in C. The only possibilities for K and C are 6 and 2, 6 and 4, and 7 and 5.

d Note that K × K ends in G. From **c** above, K can only be 6 or 7. But if K = 6, then K × K would end in K, which it does not. Hence K = 7.

e If K = 7, then C = 5 (from **c** above).

f If C = 5, then H = 0 (from **b** above).

g If K = 7, then G = 9 (since K × K ends in G).

h Look, now, at the second subtraction. In it, E − [1 (i.e. D) + the carry-over] = 0. The carry-over can only be 1; hence E − 2 = 0, making E = 2.

i Hence 7 × B7 = 259 (the last multiplication), making B = 3.

j If 5F − 37 = 21, F must = 8.

So the complete long division is:

```
        157
  37)5809
     37
     210
     185
      259
      259
      —
```

Solution 117 (Puzzle 105)

The explorer would need at least 4 bearers. Let the natives be represented by A, B, C and D and the explorer by E. The crossing might occur like this:

Day 1: A, B, C and E set out on the first 40 kilometres.

Day 2: A gives both B and E one day's rations and returns to base. B, C and E set out on the next 40 kilometres.

Day 3: C gives E a day's rations and returns to the first camp (set up at the end of day 1). B and E set out on the next 40 kilometres. In addition, A – who has returned to base – sets off with three day's rations to the first base 40 kilometres away. D also sets off for the first base, but with 4 days' rations.

Day 4: A has met up with C and gives him a day's rations. Both men return to base. B gives E a day's rations and sets off back to the second camp (80 kilometres from base). E now has sufficient supplies to complete the crossing unassisted. D sets off from the first camp bound for the second.

Day 5: E continues on his way. D, who has met up with B, shares his rations with B and both make their way to the first camp. A, with 4 days' rations, also makes his way to the first camp.

Day 6: E has only 2 days to go. A has met up with B and D, and the three return to base camp, sharing the rations A has left.

Day 7: E completes his crossing.

Solution 118 (Puzzle 87)

There are at least the following 4 solutions to this puzzle:

1	2	3	4
3	4	1	2
4	3	2	1
2	1	4	3

1	3	2	4
4	2	3	1
3	1	4	2
2	4	1	3

4	3	2	1
2	1	4	3
1	2	3	4
3	4	1	2

4	2	3	1
1	3	2	4
2	4	1	3
3	1	4	2

Solution 119 (Puzzle 100, Part A)

The two missing numbers are 7 and 11. The sequence progresses according to the following pattern:

$$+3 -1, +4 -2, +5 -3, +6 -4, \text{ and so on.}$$

Solution 120 (Puzzle 122)

Only sentence **d** is true: all others are false. You can get a start on this puzzle by considering sentence **b**. If **b** is true, then the number of true sentences—call this number N—will be 3, 4 or 5. Consider each in turn, and you will see that each yields a contradiction:

Suppose N = 3
If sentence **b** is T (true), then sentence **d** is F (false) and so must be sentence **e**. Hence **a, b** and **c** must all be true. But if **d** and **e** are F, sentence **a** must be F.

Suppose N = 4
If **b** is T, both **d** and **e** are F. Hence N, the number of true sentences, cannot be 4.

Suppose N = 5
As for the previous possibility, since **d** and **e** must be F, N cannot be greater than 3.

It follows from this that sentence **b** cannot be true. Now if **b** is F, the number of false sentences – call this number P – will be 3, 4, or 5. As before, consider each possibility in turn:

Suppose P = 3
If **b** is F and P = 3, then sentence **e** is T. Now if **d** is T, there would be two consecutive true sentences, so making **d** F. But if **d** is F, there would have to be at least 3 true sentences all in all. But then P couldn't be 3.

Suppose P = 4
If P = 4, then **a** and **e** along with **b** must be F. Sentence **d** must be T, and **c** is, then, F. All conditions set in the puzzle are met.

Suppose P = 5
If there are 5 false sentences, 4 would have to be true, making it impossible for there to be 5 false sentences!

So the only consistent possibility is that where P = 4; that is, where there are 4 false sentences, with sentence **d** the only one true.

Solution 121 (Puzzle 80)
Given the vastness of the English language, there are likely to be a number of chains of words that yield SILK as the fourth new word. Here are two:

Changing one letter at a time
    LACE   LACK   SACK   SICK   SILK

Changing two letters at a time
    LACE   LICK   PECK   WICK   SILK

Solution 122 (Puzzle 119)
The punter began with $60. Let M be the amount of money the punter started with. He put M – 30 on Hot Feet in the first race and doubled the money he had put on her. He then had 2M – 60, $30 of which he put on the favourite in the second race, and the rest, 2M – 90, on Lucky Horseshoe. Lucky Horseshoe wins, and he finds he has trebled the money he had bet on her. That is, he now has 6M – 270. In the third race, he put 6M – 300 on Bred For Speed and ended up with four times that amount, i.e. $240. So 4(6M – 300) = 240, which gives 60 as the value for M.

Solution 123 (Puzzle 121)

Colleen is 19, Dominique is 20, and Bernadette is 22. Suppose that Bernadette's one lie was that she was older than Dominique. It follows that her two other claims are true: **a** that Colleen is a year older than she is; and **b** that Dominique is 20. From **a**, it follows that Colleen's claim that she is 3 years younger than Bernadette is false, making her claim that Bernadette is 21 true. This makes Dominique's claim that Bernadette is 22 false, so making her claim that she is 19 true. But this contradicts **b** above. Suppose, instead, that Bernadette's only lie was that Dominique is 20. Her other two claims are then true: **c** that Colleen is a year older than she is; and **d** that she is older than Dominique. It follows from **c** that Colleen's claim that she is 3 years younger than Bernadette is false. It also follows that Bernadette is 21 and, from **c**, that Colleen is 22. Moreover, Colleen's claim that Dominique is older than she is would also be true, making Dominique also older than Bernadette. But this contradicts **d** above. So Bernadette's only lie was that Colleen is a year older than she is. It follows, then, that Bernadette's claim that Dominique is 20 is true. This makes Dominique's claim that she is 19 false and, in consequence, her claim that Bernadette is 22 true, as well as her claim that Colleen is a year younger than she is (i.e. 19).

Solution 124 (Puzzle 16)

The winning yacht was from France, and the best place gained by an English yacht was second. The total number of points to be awarded in the race is $9 + 8 + 7 + 6 + \ldots + 1$, which equals 45. Since the three competing countries tied, they must each have scored 15 points. Now, the only combinations of three scores totalling 15 are: 951, 942, 861, 852, 843, 762, 753 and 654. Since two of Italy's yachts were placed only after the judges had studied photographs of their finish, we can safely say that these yachts attained consecutive places. Moreover, these two yachts finished ahead of their country's third entrant. Now, the only consecutive scores in the above list with a lower third score are 762 and 654. Because 6 is common to both sets of scores, it follows that Italy must have been awarded the 6 points. Because a French yacht came last, France's scores must have been 951 or 861 (these sets of scores being the only ones to contain a 1). The latter possibility must be ruled out, since the 6 points went to Italy. Hence the 9 points went to France, giving it the winning yacht.

Since the 5 points went to France, Italy must have been awarded 762 rather than 654 points. This leaves only 843 points to be allocated to English yachts, giving England a best place of second (i.e. 8 points).

Solution 125 (Puzzle 123)

In English, the rankings are:

Bernard, Edwina, Andrew, Catherine and Davina.

In mathematics, the rankings are:

Davina, Catherine, Andrew, Edwina and Bernard.

You need to realise that since Andrew was outright dux, whoever scored higher than he did in one examination must have scored lower than he did in the other. Hence Bernard must have come fifth in mathematics if he beat Andrew in English. (The third and fourth places are taken by Andrew and Edwina.) Next, if Davina scored 15 marks more than Andrew in mathematics, she must have scored more than 15 marks *fewer* than Andrew in English (so putting her behind Catherine, who scored 15 marks fewer than Andrew in English). Now, since Catherine and Davina occupy the only available places below Andrew in English, Edwina must have come second (this being the only place left). Finally, since both places below Andrew in mathematics are taken (by Edwina and Bernard), Catherine must have scored more than Andrew. Now, if she scored 15 marks fewer than Andrew in English, Catherine must have scored fewer than 15 marks more than he did in mathematics, putting her second behind Davina, who scored 15 marks more than Andrew.

Solution 126 (Puzzle 18, Part B)

P and P are the two missing letters. There are, in fact, two combined sequences in the original sequence, one a mirror image of the other. In the first, A B D G K P V, the letters ascend the alphabet in steps increasing by one each time. In the second, Z Y W T P K E, the letters descend the alphabet in steps also increasing by one each time.

Solution 127 (Puzzle 25, Part B)

X and 8 are the missing symbols. The numbers form a series descending by 3 each time, and following each number is the letter of the alphabet that corresponds to that number if A = 1, B = 2 and so on.

Solution 128 (Puzzle 29, Part B)

TURN-OFF continues the sequence. In the first word there is an A for the first letter; in the next a B for the second letter; in the third a C for the third and so on. Only TURN-OFF has an F as the sixth letter, as it should if it is to be the sixth word in the sequence.

Solution 129 (Puzzle 56, Part B)

The two letters required are WR, making the partly spelt words:

WREN   WRONG   and   WRIGHT

Solution 130 (Puzzle 67, Part B)

J and B are the missing letters. The letters in the sequence ascend in steps of 2, 2, 2, 3, 3, 3, 4, 4, 4, 5, 5, 5 and so on.

Solution 131 (Puzzle 100, Part B)

82 should be 81, and 122 should be 121. The sequence of numbers is simply consecutive squares beginning with 8^2.

Solution 132 (Puzzle 124, Part B)

SOCCER and CHESS are the odd words out, for they refer to games, while the other 5 words refer to objectives within various games (i.e. a try in rugby, a mate in chess, a rubber in bridge, a goal in football and a run in cricket).

Solution 133 (Puzzle 72, Part B)

The missing number is 5. It helps if you ignore the spaces in this sequence. You should then see that, after the first two numbers, the rest are just the sum, in turn, of each adjacent pair of numbers (i.e. 2 + 3 = 5, 3 + 5 = 8, 5 + 8 = 13, 8 + 1 = 9 and so on).

Scorecard

The following is both a guide to the difficulty of each puzzle and a tally sheet for you to record your scores. Each puzzle has been ranked from 1 to 10, with 1 applying to the easiest puzzles and 10 to the hardest. Use the ranking as a score or mark for solving the puzzle correctly and see how close you can get to 750 – the perfect score. Those who score more than 600 have good reason to be proud and may even consider seeking membership to one or other of the societies for the intellectually gifted, such as:

- Mensa – for those with an IQ in the top 2%
- Intertel – for those in the top 1%
- Triple Nine Society – for those in the top 0.1%.

Puzzle	Ranking	Mark	Puzzle	Ranking	Mark
1	5		20	4	
2	5		21	4	
3	7		22	5	
4	4		23	3	
5	10		24	4	
6	5		25a	4	
7	4		25b	5	
8	3		26	6	
9	3		27	5	
10	3		28	4	
11	4		29a	4	
12	4		29b	4	
13	5		30	4	
14	4		31	6	
15	5		32	9	
16	9		33	4	
17	3		34	4	
18a	4		35	4	
18b	5		36	6	
19	5		37	4	
Sub-total			**Sub-total**		

Puzzle	Ranking	Mark
38	9	
39	5	
40	6	
41	9	
42	8	
43	8	
44	10	
45	4	
46	7	
47	3	
48	4	
49	4	
50	3	
51	4	
52	4	
53	7	
54	6	
55	7	
56a	3	
56b	4	
57	6	
58	6	
59	6	
60	5	
61	3	
62	10	
63	7	
64	6	
65	4	
66	9	
67a	4	
67b	4	
68	7	
69	4	
Sub-total		

Puzzle	Ranking	Mark
70	8	
71	7	
72a	3	
72b	4	
73	6	
74	6	
75	4	
76	4	
77	6	
78	6	
79	4	
80	5	
81	4	
82	6	
83	5	
84	6	
85	10	
86	6	
87	6	
88	8	
89	5	
90	8	
91	6	
92	10	
93	10	
94	7	
95	9	
96	7	
97	5	
98	3	
99	4	
100a	4	
100b	4	
101	8	
Sub-total		

Puzzle	Ranking	Mark
102	6	
103	5	
104	5	
105	8	
106	8	
107	4	
108	3	
109	8	
110	10	
111	5	
112	4	
113	9	
114	7	
115	5	
116	4	
117	7	
118	7	
119	6	
120	5	
121	8	
122	10	
123	7	
124a	5	
124b	5	
125	9	

Sub-total _____

Total Score = _____ marks out of 750